# Cheesecakes Pavlovas
## and Luscious Desserts

### The Family Circle® Promise of Success

Welcome to the world of Confident Cooking,
created for you in the Australian **Family Circle®
Test Kitchen,** where recipes are double-tested by
our team of home economists to achieve a
high standard of success—and delicious
results every time.

**MURDOCH BOOKS®**
Sydney • London • Vancouver • New York

# C O N T E

Liqueur Coffee Cheesecake, page 27

Red Wine Jelly with Frosted Fruits, page 73

Golden Apple Cheesecake, page 35

Fluffy Pavlova, page 43

Chocolate Collar Cheesecake, page 32

Triple Chocolate Terrine, page 98

The Publisher thanks the following for their assistance in the photography for this book: Waterford Wedgwood; Rosenthal; Orson and Blake Collectables; South Pacific Fabrics; Country Affair; Gein; Cydonia—The Glass Studio; Incorporated Agencies.
**Front cover:** Strawberry Cream Meringue Gateau (page 47), Citrus Cheesecake (page 30) and Berry Nests (page 46)
**Inside front cover:** Fresh Fruit Pavlova (page 37)

All recipes in this book have been double-tested.

When we test our recipes, we rate them for ease of preparation. The following cookery ratings are on the recipes in this book, making them easy to use and understand.

A single Cooking with Confidence symbol indicates a recipe that is simple and generally quick to make – perfect for beginners.

Two symbols indicate the need for just a little more care and a little more time.

Three symbols indicate special dishes that need more investment in time, care and patience—but the results are worth it.

### NOTES
International conversions and a glossary explaining unfamiliar terms can be found on page 112. Cooking times may vary slightly depending on the individual oven. We suggest you check the manufacturer's instructions to ensure proper temperature control.

Vanilla Bavarois, page 108

Pears with Ginger Zabaglione, page 85

# Hints and Secrets

Why do your cheesecakes sag in the middle? Why do your egg whites never whisk up to perfection? And why doesn't your chocolate terrine make your friends sob with envy? The difference between a good dessert and a truly mouthwatering masterpiece often lies in those little secrets that clever cooks keep to themselves. Here are a few hints to help you on your way to a professional finish.

### PREPARING THE TIN

The golden rule is... always measure across the base. The top of the tin is often a little wider than the base so, if your results aren't always perfect, you may be using the wrong sized tin.

There are several simple ways to quickly prepare the tin. One is to grease the tin lightly with a little melted butter or oil (you can also use the commercial greasing sprays) then dust it with a small amount of flour. Shake out the excess by tapping the tin to dislodge any loose flour. This is quick and efficient but not absolutely guaranteed to prevent sticking.

A safer way, and the one that we prefer to use, is the greasing and lining method. Grease the tin as above and then line it with baking paper. (It is not always necessary to line the sides as well as the base.) Baking paper has a silicone coating, which will usually prevent sticking. If you use greaseproof paper, you then have to grease the paper after lining. Cut one long or two shorter lengths, long enough to fit around the tin and about 4 cm higher than the rim. Make diagonal cuts at intervals along one side and then ease the lining into the tin to fit snugly. Place a sheet in the base, cut to whatever shape you need.

For a swiss roll tin, place the tin on a sheet of baking paper and mark with a pencil where the base corners are. Cut into these corners and then ease the paper into the greased tin, smoothing out any air bubbles.

### BAKING BLIND

Baking blind ensures that the pastry base is cooked thoroughly and is not soggy. Prepare the pastry and ease it into the tin. Lay a sheet of baking paper over the pastry, large enough to cover the base and sides. Spread a layer of rice, dried beans or baking beads over the paper. Bake in a preheated oven for however long the recipe tells you, then remove the paper and rice, beans or beads. Bake for a little longer, as specified, until the pastry is golden. Baking beads can be bought from department stores and speciality kitchen shops but a cheaper alternative is chickpeas, which, like the rice or beans, can be stored in a separate jar and re-used.

### TESTING YOUR CHEESECAKE

It is often difficult to tell whether your cheesecake is cooked properly. A simple test is to gently wobble it. This should be done with the oven door slightly ajar, leaving the cheesecake in the oven. Taking the cheesecake out of the oven may cause it to sink if it isn't cooked properly. The cheesecake should have a slight wobble in the middle. The remaining heat left in the cheesecake will be enough to set it—if completely set, it may crack on cooling and has probably been overcooked. It is always best to cool the cheesecake completely and then refrigerate it overnight—this will give you a firm cheesecake that has a rich and creamy texture.

### SECRETS OF THE PERFECT MERINGUE

To make meringue use a clean, dry mixing bowl and, if possible, electric beaters. If you don't have electric beaters, rotating balloon beaters or a large hand whisk will suffice, but you'll need a little more elbow grease. It is best to have your egg whites at room temperature and preferable to use caster sugar as it dissolves faster than any of the larger crystal sugars. Beat the egg whites to soft, firm or stiff peaks as the recipe requires. The aim is to reach maximum volume, without overbeating. Gradually add the sugar, usually about 1 tablespoon at a time unless the recipe says otherwise. Beat well after each addition to dissolve the sugar. Scrape down the sides of the bowl with a spatula while you beat, to incorporate all the sugar. When you think the meringue is ready, take a little mixture and rub it between your thumb and forefinger. It should feel smooth and slightly gritty. If the mixture feels very gritty it needs extra beating.

*Make diagonal cuts along one edge of the paper so it fits snugly into the base of tin.*

*If the sugar has not fully dissolved the mixture will still feel very gritty.*

There are several different methods for making meringues and some will require you to add a little sugar at the end of beating. In this case, do not beat the mixture again to dissolve the sugar. Another method is to heat the sugar and egg white together for about 10 minutes, or until thick and glossy. The rubbing test can be used for this.

## DECORATING

### Crazy for Chocolate
Chocolate has endless uses for decorating. With a little imagination, you can create simple designs which actually look as if you have laboured over them for hours.
*Chocolate Lattice:* Melt about 60 g of dark, white or milk chocolate and spoon it into a small paper icing bag. Seal the end and snip off the pointed tip. Pipe the lattice roughly onto sheets of baking paper. Allow to set, then carefully peel away from the paper. Compound chocolate or chocolate melts will set at room temperature rather quickly. Couverture or cooking chocolate will take much longer and may need refrigeration, although the taste is preferable.

*Pipe melted chocolate in a criss-cross pattern onto the baking paper.*

*Chocolate Leaves:* Choose a selection of non-toxic leaves with interesting shapes and prominent veins on the underside. (Try not to pick furry leaves, as the fibres stick to the chocolate when the leaf is peeled away. They also leave the chocolate with a dull finish.) Melt about 60 g of chocolate and use a fine brush to paint it over the underside of the leaf. Leave to set then peel away the leaf. If the coating of chocolate is too thin, it will break when the leaf is removed.

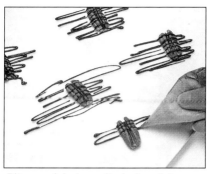

*Pipe or drizzle melted chocolate over pecans or other nuts for decoration.*

*Chocolate Nuts:* Dip nuts in melted chocolate or drizzle the chocolate over them and allow to set on foil.

### Candied Citrus Rind and Slices
Use any citrus fruit you like for this.
*Candied Rind:* Peel long strips around the fruit, not from top to base. Take care not to peel off too much of the white pith—a very sharp knife is essential. Remove any white pith still attached and then cut the rind into long, thin strips. You can also use a special 'zester', however you may find it difficult to scrape really long strips. Combine 1 cup sugar and 1/3 cup water in a pan. Stir over low heat without boiling until the sugar dissolves. Bring to the boil, then reduce the heat and simmer the rind in batches for about 5 minutes or until transparent. Remove with tongs and drain until cooled.
*Candied Slices:* Slice the fruit very thinly and add it to the simmering syrup in batches. Cook for about 5–10 minutes or until transparent and toffee-like, then remove and cool. Add an extra 1/3 cup of sugar to the syrup between batches and stir gently to dissolve—the juice from the fruit breaks down the concentrated syrup and the fruit won't candy properly unless you add more sugar.

### Spectacular Toffee Toppings
It is not wise to try to make toffee on a humid day. Humidity causes the toffee to break down and liquefy, so instead of setting it will become sticky and wet. Putting it in the refrigerator will only accelerate the problem. But don't let this put you off—on the right day, it's well worth the effort.

Toffee can be used in a variety of ways. Whole roasted nuts can be dipped in toffee and left on a foil- or baking paper-lined tray to set. Choux puffs can be dipped in toffee to stick them together.

Spinning toffee is really quite simple, once you've practised a little. Allow it to cool slightly then take two forks and dip the ends in the toffee. Rub the backs together until the toffee begins to stick. Gently pull the forks apart to check whether the toffee is cool enough to spin. If it drips or dips it probably needs a little longer to cool. If not, continue pulling the toffee apart and wrap it around the dessert, pressing the forks together to spin a second time when they meet. Re-dip the forks and continue spinning backwards and forwards. You can also spin toffee around a greased jar, allow it to set and then use to decorate.

*Rub the backs of the forks together until the toffee is tacky then gently pull apart.*

*Spin fine lengths of toffee around, pressing the forks together when they meet.*

### Sugared Flowers and Leaves
Choose a selection of edible flowers and leaves (rose petals and violets always look stunning), gently rinse them and pat dry. Brush them carefully with lightly beaten egg white, then sprinkle with a little caster sugar and shake off the excess. Set aside to dry before using.

# CHEESE-CAKES

## NEW YORK CHEESECAKE

Preparation time: 1 hour + chilling
Total cooking time: 1 hour 50 minutes
Serves 10–12

1/2 cup self-raising flour
1 cup plain flour
1/4 cup caster sugar
1 teaspoon grated lemon rind
80 g butter
1 egg

*Filling*
750 g cream cheese, softened
1 cup caster sugar
1/4 cup plain flour
2 teaspoons grated orange rind
2 teaspoons grated lemon rind
4 eggs
2/3 cup cream

*Candied Rind*
1 cup caster sugar
rind of 3 limes, 3 lemons and
    3 oranges, shredded
1 1/2 cups cream

**1** Process the flours, sugar, lemon rind and butter for 30 seconds, or until crumbly. Add the egg and process until the mixture just comes together. Knead gently on a floured surface, wrap in plastic wrap and refrigerate for 20 minutes, or until firm.

**2** Preheat the oven to hot 210°C. Roll the pastry between 2 sheets of baking paper until large enough to fit the base and side of a greased 22.5 cm or 23 cm round springform cake tin. Ease into the tin and trim the edges. Bake blind for 10 minutes, remove the baking paper and beans, flatten the pastry lightly with the back of a spoon and bake for 5 minutes. Cool.

**3 To make the Filling:** Reduce the oven to 150°C. Beat the cream cheese, sugar, flour and rinds until smooth. Add the eggs, one at a time, beating after each addition. Beat in the cream, pour the filling over the pastry and bake for 1 hour 25–35 minutes, or until almost set. Cool, then refrigerate.

**4 To make the Candied Rind:** Put the sugar in a pan with 1/4 cup water and stir over low heat until dissolved. Add the rind, bring to the boil, reduce the heat and simmer for 5–6 minutes. Allow to cool and drain the rind (you can save the syrup to serve with the cheesecake). Whip the cream, spoon over the cold cheesecake and top with Candied Rind.

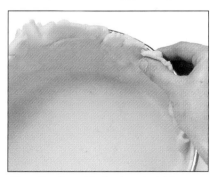

*Line the tin with pastry, patching any tears if necessary.*

*Add the shredded rind to the sugar syrup and bring to the boil.*

## PASSIONFRUIT CHEESECAKE SLICE

Preparation time: 30 minutes +
 6 hours chilling
Total cooking time: Nil
Makes about 20 slices

250 g butternut cookies
90 g butter, melted
2 teaspoons gelatine
250 g ricotta cheese
250 g cream cheese, softened
400 g can condensed milk
2 teaspoons grated lemon rind
1/4 cup lemon juice

3/4 cup thickened cream,
 whipped to soft peaks
pulp of 6 passionfruit
extra whipped cream and
 passionfruit pulp, to decorate

**1** Brush a 30 x 20 cm tin with melted butter or oil and line with non-stick baking paper. Process the biscuits in a food processor for 20 seconds, or until finely crushed. Stir in the butter until well combined. Spoon into the tin, pressing firmly into the base. Chill while you prepare the filling.
**2** Put 1/4 cup water in a small heat-proof bowl. Sprinkle with gelatine and put in a slightly larger bowl of boiling water; stir and then leave to dissolve. Leave to cool slightly. Beat the ricotta and cream cheese with electric beaters for 3 minutes, until softened and smooth. Add the condensed milk, lemon rind and juice and continue to beat for 2–3 minutes, until well mixed.
**3** Fold in the cream, gelatine and passionfruit pulp. Pour into the tin and smooth. Refrigerate for 6 hours, or until firm. Cut into squares and lift out of the tin. Decorate with a little extra passionfruit pulp and cream.

### COOK'S FILE

**Storage time:** Cover and refrigerate for up to three days. Do not freeze.

*Press the crumb base into the lined tin with a spoon.*

*Sprinkle gelatine over the water gradually, letting it soften between additions.*

*Fold in the cream, gelatine and passion-fruit pulp with a metal spoon.*

# BAKED CHOCOLATE CHEESECAKE

Preparation time: 20 minutes +
  overnight chilling
Total cooking time: 1 hour 25 minutes
Serves 8–10

125 g plain chocolate biscuits
1/4 cup chopped almonds
90 g butter, melted
1 tablespoon soft brown sugar

*Filling*
500 g cream cheese, at
  room temperature
1/2 cup soft brown sugar
125 g dark chocolate, melted
1/2 cup thickened cream
2 eggs, beaten
1 teaspoon grated orange rind

**1** Brush a 20 cm round springform tin with melted butter or oil and line the base with non-stick baking paper. Put the biscuits in a food processor with the almonds and process into crumbs. Add the butter and sugar and process again until well combined. Press firmly into the base of the tin and refrigerate until firm. Preheat the oven to 160°C.

**2 To make the Filling:** Beat the cream cheese and sugar together until the mixture is creamy. Blend in the cooled melted chocolate, cream, eggs and orange rind and then mix until smooth. Pour the filling over the crumb crust and smooth the surface. Bake for 1 hour 20–25 minutes, or until the filling is firm to the touch.

**3** Leave the cheesecake to cool in the tin and then refrigerate overnight. Delicious topped with whipped cream, fresh raspberries and chocolate curls.

**COOK'S FILE**

**Note:** The filling can be made in a food processor. The melted chocolate should be at the same temperature as the rest of the ingredients when it is added, otherwise lumps may form. Add 1–2 tablespoons Grand Marnier to the filling for a special occasion and serve topped with whipped cream and caramelised oranges.

*Brush the tin with oil or melted butter and line the base with baking paper.*

*Add the butter and sugar to the crushed biscuit almond mix.*

*Blend the chocolate, cream, orange rind and eggs into the mixture.*

# Bistro Cheesecake

### BASIC CHEESECAKE RECIPE

**To make the base:** Brush a 20 cm round springform tin with melted butter or oil and line the base with non-stick baking paper. Finely crush 250 g butternut cookies and stir in 1 teaspoon mixed spice and 100 g melted butter until well combined. Spoon into the tin, pressing firmly over the base and side. Refrigerate for 20 minutes, or until firm.

**To make the filling:** Preheat the oven to 180°C. Beat 500 g cream cheese with electric beaters until smooth. Add $2/3$ cup caster sugar, 1 teaspoon vanilla essence and 1 tablespoon lemon juice and beat until smooth. Add 4 eggs, one at a time, beating well after each addition. Pour over the crust and bake for 45–50 minutes, or until just firm.

**To make the topping:** Mix together 1 cup sour cream, $1/2$ teaspoon vanilla essence, 3 teaspoons lemon juice and 1 tablespoon caster sugar in a bowl. Carefully spread over the hot cheesecake. Sprinkle with ground nutmeg and return to the oven for a further 7 minutes. Allow to cool and refrigerate until firm. Will serve 8–10 people.

Bistro Cheesecake has a soft creamy centre and can be made without the sour cream topping but will then need to be cooked for a further 5–10 minutes. The beauty of a basic baked cheesecake recipe is that it can be decorated with a huge variety of toppings depending on the occasion.

### Golden Mango

Heat 30 g butter, $1/4$ cup soft brown sugar, 2 tablespoons apricot jam and 1 tablespoon Grand Marnier in a large non-stick frying pan. Stir over low heat until the sugar has dissolved. Add 2 large peeled and thinly sliced mangoes and simmer gently for 3–4 minutes, but don't allow the mango to become mushy. Cool almost completely, then arrange the mango slices on top of the cheesecake while it is still in the tin. Reduce any remaining syrup by simmering for a further 2–3 minutes, then brush or drizzle over the mango. Chill for about an hour in the tin.

### Indulgent Strawberries and Cream

Omit the sour cream topping. Whip $1^{1}/4$ cups cream to firm peaks and carefully release the cooled cheesecake from its tin. Spoon cream over the cheesecake and decorate with fresh halved or whole strawberries. Spoon over the pulp of 2 passionfruit or simply dust with a little icing sugar.

*From top: Basic Cheesecake; Golden Mango; Indulgent Strawberries and Cream; Caramel*

## Caramel

Put 60 g butter, 1/4 cup soft or dark brown sugar, 1/2 cup condensed milk and 1/2 cup cream in a pan and stir over low heat until the butter has melted and the sugar dissolved. Bring to the boil, reduce the heat and simmer gently for 5–10 minutes, stirring continuously to prevent the caramel catching on the bottom of the pan. Remove from the heat, cool almost completely and then carefully spread over the cheesecake while still in the tin. Refrigerate in the tin for about an hour, or until just set.

## Double Chocolate

Fold 1/3 cup dark choc bits into the cheesecake filling before baking. Omit the sour cream topping and allow the cheesecake to cool. Put 200 g dark chopped chocolate and 1/3 cup sour cream in a pan and whisk over low heat until the chocolate has melted and the mixture is smooth. Leave to cool slightly, then spread evenly over the cheesecake while still in the tin. Refrigerate until set, release from the tin and decorate with white, milk and dark chocolate curls.

## Rich Cherry

Drain a large can or jar of pitted sour cherries and leave on paper towels to absorb any remaining juice. Arrange the cherries over the cheesecake while it is still in the tin. Put 2/3 cup sieved blackberry or mulberry jam and 2–3 tablespoons kirsch or cherry brandy in a small pan and simmer over low heat for 2–3 minutes, or until smooth and a little reduced. Cool slightly, then brush liberally over the cherries. It may be necessary to reheat the jam if it begins to thicken quickly. The setting time depends on the consistency of the jam used. Allow to set before removing from the tin.

## Blueberry Marmalade

Combine 1/2 cup water, 1 cup caster sugar and 2 tablespoons lemon or lime juice in a pan and stir over low heat without boiling until the sugar has completely dissolved. Add 400 g blueberries and 4 cinnamon sticks. Bring to the boil, reduce the heat and simmer for about 15 minutes, or until reduced and thickened. Leave to cool slightly and then serve spooned over wedges of cheesecake.

## Fruit Salad Frenzy

Arrange thin slices of fresh kiwi fruit, halved strawberries, fresh whole blueberries, thin slices of mango and halved black and green grapes over the top of the cheesecake. Heat a jar of fruit salad baby gel in a small pan and add 2–3 teaspoons brandy. Simmer for 1–2 minutes and then brush over the fruit on the cheesecake. Allow to set before removing from the tin. (Canned fruits need to be well drained. The extra liquid in these may begin to weep and discolour the cheesecake if left to stand for too long.)

*From top: Double Chocolate; Rich Cherry;*
*Blueberry Marmalade; Fruit Salad Frenzy*

## BUTTERMILK CHEESECAKE WITH RASPBERRY SAUCE

Preparation time: 35 minutes + chilling
Total cooking time: 1 hour 20 minutes
   to 2 hours
Serves 8

250 g granita biscuits
125 g butter, melted
3 teaspoons grated lemon rind
750 g ricotta cheese
4 eggs, lightly beaten
1 cup buttermilk
2 tablespoons cornflour
1/2 cup honey
1 tablespoon lemon juice
icing sugar, to dust

*Raspberry Sauce*
300 g packet frozen raspberries
1/4 cup icing sugar
1 teaspoon lemon juice

**1** Brush a 22.5 cm or 23 cm round springform tin with melted butter or oil and line the base with non-stick baking paper. Preheat the oven to 160°C. Put the biscuits in a food processor and process for 20 seconds, or until finely crushed. Stir in the melted butter and 2 teaspoons of the lemon rind until combined. Spoon into the tin and press firmly over the base. Refrigerate, then prepare the filling.
**2** Beat the ricotta with electric beaters for 2 minutes, or until smooth; add the eggs gradually, beating well after each addition. Whisk together the buttermilk and cornflour until smooth and add gradually to the ricotta mixture. Beat in the honey, remaining lemon rind and juice. Pour into the tin. Bake for about 1 hour

20 minutes, or until set (this may take up to 2 hours, depending on your oven). Cool, then refrigerate for at least 6 hours. Bring to room temperature to serve. Dust with icing sugar and serve with Raspberry Sauce.
**3 To make Raspberry Sauce:** Defrost the raspberries and process with the icing sugar for 20 seconds, or until smooth. Add lemon juice to taste.

### COOK'S FILE

**Storage time:** Cover and refrigerate for up to three days but do not freeze.

*When the ricotta is smooth, continue to beat, gradually adding the eggs.*

*Pour the filling mixture over the base in the tin.*

*Process the icing sugar and defrosted raspberries until smooth.*

## SWEET PUMPKIN CHEESECAKE

Preparation time: 40 minutes +
  6 hours chilling
Total cooking time: 1 hour 40 minutes
Serves 8–10

185 g wheatmeal biscuits
90 g butter, melted
600 g pumpkin, cubed
250 g cream cheese, softened
500 g ricotta cheese
1/2 cup honey
2 tablespoons cornflour

1 teaspoon ground nutmeg, plus
  extra for sprinkling
3 eggs, lightly beaten
1 cup cream, whipped

**1** Brush a 23 cm round springform tin with melted butter or oil and line the base with non-stick baking paper. Process the biscuits for 20 seconds, or until finely crushed. Stir in the butter until well combined. Spoon into the tin and press evenly and firmly over the base. Refrigerate while you prepare the filling. Preheat the oven to 150°C.
**2** Microwave or boil the pumpkin until tender. Drain, cool and purée.

Beat the cream cheese and ricotta with electric beaters for 3 minutes, or until smooth. Add the pumpkin, honey, cornflour and 1 teaspoon nutmeg and beat for 2–3 minutes, until smooth.
**3** Add the egg a tablespoon at a time, mixing well. Pour into the tin and smooth. Bake for 1 1/2 hours, or until firm to the touch. Cool completely in the tin, spread with cream and sprinkle with a little extra nutmeg. Chill for 6 hours. Serve with custard.

### COOK'S FILE

**Storage time:** Cover and refrigerate for up to three days but do not freeze.

*Microwave or boil the pumpkin cubes in water until tender.*

*Add the pumpkin purée, honey, cornflour and nutmeg and beat.*

*Smooth the surface of the filling with the back of a spoon.*

# BRANDY CHEESECAKE

Preparation time: 35 minutes +
  6 hours chilling
Total cooking time: 30 minutes
Serves 8–10

250 g granita biscuits
100 g butter, melted
1 teaspoon cinnamon
500 g cream cheese, softened
1/2 cup sour cream
1/2 cup caster sugar
2 eggs
2 tablespoons custard powder
1 tablespoon lemon juice
1 teaspoon grated lemon rind
2 tablespoons brandy
1/2 cup sultanas

*Topping*
300 ml cream, whipped
1/4 cup icing sugar
1/2 teaspoon ground ginger
1/2 teaspoon ground cinnamon

**1** Brush the base and two long sides of a 30 x 20 cm tin with melted butter or oil and line with non-stick baking paper. Preheat the oven to 160°C. Put the biscuits in a food processor and process for 20 seconds, or until finely crushed. Stir in the melted butter and cinnamon until well combined. Spoon into the tin, pressing firmly and evenly into the base. Refrigerate while you prepare the filling.
**2** Beat the cream cheese and sour cream for 3 minutes, or until smooth. Add the sugar in batches and beat for a further 2 minutes. Add the eggs, one at a time, beating for 2–3 minutes until well mixed.
**3** Beat in the custard powder, lemon juice, lemon rind and brandy. Stir in the sultanas. Spoon into the tin and smooth. Bake for 30 minutes, or until set. Cool and then refrigerate for at least 6 hours or overnight.
**4** **To make the Topping:** Combine the cream, sugar and spices. Just before serving spread evenly over the cake. Alternatively, spoon a little cream over individual servings and sprinkle with spices.

### COOK'S FILE

**Storage time:** Keeps, refrigerated without cream, for up to three days.

*Line the greased tin with a sheet of non-stick baking paper.*

*Mix the biscuits in a food processor until they are finely crushed.*

*Add the sugar in batches, beating after each addition.*

*Gently stir the sultanas into the mixture before spooning into the tin.*

# BLUEBERRY CHEESECAKE

Preparation time: 40 minutes + chilling
Total cooking time: 45–50 minutes
Serves 8–10

125 g butter
1 cup rolled oats
100 g wheatmeal biscuits,
    finely crushed
2 tablespoons soft brown sugar

*Filling*
375 g light cream cheese
100 g fresh ricotta cheese
1/3 cup caster sugar
1/2 cup sour cream
2 eggs
1 tablespoon finely grated
    orange rind
1 tablespoon plain flour

*Topping*
250 g fresh blueberries
3/4 cup blackberry spreadable
    fruit or conserve
1/4 cup cherry brandy

**1** Brush a 20 cm round, deep spring-form tin with melted butter or oil and line the base with non-stick baking paper. Melt the butter in a pan, add the oats and biscuit crumbs and mix well. Stir in the sugar. Press half the biscuit mixture into the base of the tin and gradually press the rest around the side, to about 2 cm below the rim, using a glass to firm it into place. Refrigerate for 10–15 minutes. Preheat the oven to moderate 180°C.

**2 To make the Filling:** Beat the cream cheese, ricotta, sugar and sour cream with electric beaters until smooth. Beat in the eggs, rind and flour until smooth. Pour into the crust, put the tin on a flat oven tray to catch any drips and bake for 40–50 minutes, or until just set. Remove from the oven but leave in the tin to cool. If you have time, it is best to refrigerate the cheesecake overnight.

**3 To make the Topping:** Scatter the blueberries on top of the cheesecake. Sieve the spreadable fruit or conserve into a pan with the brandy. Stir over medium heat until smooth and then simmer for 2–3 minutes. Carefully brush over the blueberries.

*Use a glass to press the biscuit mixture into the base and around the side.*

*Bake the cheesecake on a flat oven tray to catch any overflow.*

*Sieve the spreadable fruit or conserve into a pan with the brandy.*

## CHOCOLATE JAFFA CHEESECAKE

Preparation time: 45 minutes +
6 hours chilling
Total cooking time: Nil
Serves 6–8

125 g granita biscuits
60 g butter, melted
2 teaspoons gelatine
250 g cream cheese, softened
1/4 cup icing sugar
150 g dark chocolate, melted
1/2 cup chocolate
hazelnut spread
2 teaspoons grated orange rind

2 tablespoons Cointreau or
Grand Marnier
300 ml thickened cream,
whipped to soft peaks
300 ml cream, whipped

**1** Brush a 20 cm round springform tin with melted butter or oil and line the base with non-stick baking paper. Finely crush the biscuits in a food processor for 20 seconds. Stir in the butter until well combined. Spoon into the tin, pressing firmly over the base. Refrigerate while you make the filling.
**2** Put 1/4 cup water in a small heat-proof bowl. Sprinkle with gelatine and then stand this in a larger bowl of very hot water. Stir and leave to

dissolve. Cool slightly. Beat the cream cheese for 3 minutes, or until softened and smooth. Beat in the icing sugar. Add the gelatine, chocolate, 1/4 cup chocolate spread, orange rind and liqueur. Beat for 2–3 minutes, or until well mixed and an even colour.
**3** Fold in the thickened cream with a metal spoon. Spoon over the base and smooth. Chill for at least 6 hours. Soften the remaining chocolate spread with a little cream. Fold in the rest of the cream and spoon over the cheesecake. Top with chocolate curls, if liked.

**COOK'S FILE**

**Storage time:** Cover and refrigerate for up to three days. Do not freeze.

*Sprinkle the gelatine over a bowl of water standing in a larger bowl of hot water.*

*Add the icing sugar to the softened cream cheese and beat well.*

*Use a metal spoon to lightly fold in the cream until it is mixed through.*

## LEMON HONEY CHEESECAKE

Preparation time: 40 minutes +
overnight chilling
Total cooking time: Nil
Serves 6–8

250 g honey snap biscuits
1 1/2 teaspoons mixed spice
125 g butter, melted
375 g cream cheese, softened

1 tablespoon grated lemon rind
2 teaspoons vanilla essence
400 g can condensed milk
1/3 cup lemon juice

**1** Brush a 20 cm round springform tin with melted butter or oil and line the base with non-stick baking paper. Put the biscuits in a food processor and finely crush. Stir in the spice and melted butter until all the crumbs are moistened. Press half the biscuit mixture into the base of the tin and

gradually press the remainder around the sides, using a glass to firm it into place. Refrigerate for 10–15 minutes.
**2** Beat the cream cheese until smooth and creamy. Add the lemon rind and vanilla essence and beat to combine. Gradually beat in the condensed milk and lemon juice. Beat for 5 minutes, or until smooth and increased in volume.
**3** Pour onto the biscuit base and smooth. Refrigerate overnight. If you like, decorate with freshly whipped cream and slices of candied lemon.

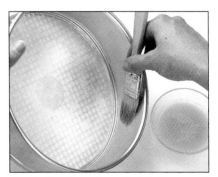

*Brush the tin with melted butter or oil and line the base with non-stick paper.*

*Press half the biscuit mixture into the base of the tin with a spoon.*

*Gradually beat in the condensed milk and lemon juice.*

*Chocolate Jaffa Cheesecake (top) and
Lemon Honey Cheesecake*

## RUM AND RAISIN CHEESECAKE

Preparation time: 40 minutes
Total cooking time: 1 hour 10 minutes
Serves 10–12

**125 g plain sweet biscuits**
**1/4 cup chopped pecans**
**90 g butter, melted**

*Filling*
**750 g cream cheese, softened**
**1/2 cup caster sugar**
**2 tablespoons dark rum**
**3 eggs, separated**
**300 g sour cream**

**1 tablespoon plain flour**
**1/2 cup raisins**
**ground nutmeg**

**1** Brush a 23 cm round springform tin with melted butter or oil and line the base with non-stick baking paper. Put the biscuits in a food processor with the pecans and process into crumbs. Add the butter and process until well combined. Press into the base of the tin and refrigerate until firm. Preheat the oven to 160°C.
**2 To make the Filling:** Beat the cream cheese until soft. Gradually beat in the sugar, then the rum. Add the egg yolks, one at a time, beating well after each addition. Beat in the

sour cream and flour. Fold in the raisins. Beat the egg whites until stiff peaks form and fold lightly into the filling. Pour the filling over the prepared crumb crust. Smooth and sprinkle lightly with nutmeg.
**3** Bake for about 1 hour 10 minutes, or until firm to the touch. Allow the cheesecake to cool in the oven, then refrigerate. Try serving with whipped cream and shaved chocolate.

### COOK'S FILE

**Hint:** Beat egg whites in a clean, dry bowl with clean beaters for optimum volume. Don't do this until you are ready to use them as once beaten they break down quickly.

*Put the biscuits and pecans in a food processor and process into crumbs.*

*Add the egg yolks gradually, beating well after each addition.*

*Beat the egg whites in a clean, dry bowl until soft peaks form.*

# TROPICAL CHEESECAKE

Preparation time: 50 minutes +
overnight chilling
Total cooking time: Nil
Serves 8

145 g plain sweet biscuits
1/4 cup desiccated coconut
90 g butter, melted
1/2 cup fresh orange juice
6 teaspoons gelatine
350 g cream cheese, softened
1/3 cup caster sugar
2 tablespoons lemon juice
425 g can mangoes,
    drained and chopped

450 g can unsweetened crushed
    pineapple, drained
300 ml thickened cream
extra whipped cream, kiwi
    fruit and mango wedges,
    to decorate

**1** Brush a 20 cm round springform tin with melted butter or oil and line the base with non-stick baking paper. Put the biscuits in a food processor and process for 20 seconds, or until crumbly. Add the coconut and butter and process until well combined. Spoon into the tin and press evenly and firmly over the base. Refrigerate.
**2** Put the orange juice in a small heatproof bowl and sprinkle with gelatine. Stand the bowl over a dish of boiling water, stir and then leave to dissolve. Beat the cream cheese and sugar for 3 minutes, or until smooth. Beat in the lemon juice and gently fold in the mango and pineapple. Fold in the dissolved gelatine.
**3** Lightly whip the cream into firm peaks. Fold into the mixture with a metal spoon. Pour into the tin, smooth and chill overnight. Decorate with extra cream and slices of fruit.

COOK'S FILE

**Hint:** If in season, you can use two fresh mangoes instead of the tinned. Peel, seed and chop them, increasing the caster sugar to 1/2 cup.

*Finely crush the biscuits in a food processor and then add the coconut.*

*Gently fold the mango and pineapple into the filling mixture.*

*Lightly whip the thickened cream until firm peaks form.*

## RASPBERRY CHEESECAKE

Preparation time: 1 hour 30 minutes + overnight chilling
Total cooking time: 20–25 minutes
Serves 6–8

150 g plain sweet biscuits, finely crushed
70 g butter, melted
250 g cream cheese, softened
1/3 cup + 1 teaspoon castor sugar
2/3 cup sour cream
2 eggs, separated
1 teaspoon cornflour
2/3 cup milk
2 teaspoons vanilla essence
1 tablespoon gelatine
300 g frozen/fresh raspberries
1/3 cup raspberry jam, sieved
2 tablespoons brandy

*Sponge Collar*
2 eggs, separated
1/3 cup caster sugar
1/3 cup self-raising flour
2 tablespoons cornflour
20 g butter, melted

**1** Brush a 20 cm round springform tin with melted butter or oil and line the base with non-stick baking paper. Combine the biscuits and melted butter in a bowl and stir until the biscuits are moistened. Press firmly into the base of the tin and refrigerate.
**2** To make the filling, beat the cream cheese, 1/3 cup sugar and the sour cream until smooth and creamy. Whisk together the remaining sugar, egg yolks and cornflour until thick and pale. Heat the milk until almost boiling and then whisk gradually into the yolk mixture. Return the mixture to the pan and stir over low heat until the mixture thickens and coats the back of a wooden spoon. Remove from the heat; stir in the vanilla essence. Put plastic wrap over the surface and allow to cool slightly. Sprinkle the gelatine over 1 tablespoon of boiling water in a small bowl; stand this in a basin of hot water and stir until dissolved. Stir into the custard. Fold the custard into the cream cheese mixture, stirring until smooth. Beat the egg whites until firm peaks form

and gently fold into the filling. Fold in the raspberries—do not overmix, or they may break up. Spoon over the crust and refrigerate overnight.
**3 To make the Sponge Collar:** Line the base of a 25 x 38 cm baking tin with non-stick baking paper. Mark 2 parallel lines on the paper, 8 cm apart, then mark another set the same. Allow plenty of space between the two sets of lines, so that the sponges don't touch when cooking. Preheat the oven to 180°C. Beat the egg whites with electric beaters until firm peaks form and gradually add the sugar, beating well after each addition. Continue beating until glossy and the sugar has dissolved. Beat in the yolks. Use a metal spoon to fold in the sifted combined flours, a third at a time. Gently fold in the butter until smooth.
**4** Spoon the sponge mixture into a piping bag, fitted with a 1 cm plain round nozzle, and pipe in a close snaking pattern between the marked lines. Bake for 10–15 minutes, or until lightly browned. Leave on the tray to cool. Carefully remove the cheesecake from the tin. Trim a long side and ends of each sponge and carefully wrap around the cheesecake with the flat edge on the base. Press gently to make the collar stick to the cheesecake, or tie with a ribbon.
**5** Heat the jam and brandy in a small pan and simmer over low heat for 2–3 minutes, or until reduced slightly. Allow to cool a little before brushing very gently over the top of the cheesecake, making sure not to tear the top. Allow to set before serving.

### COOK'S FILE

**Note:** The sponge collar can be made up to 12 hours in advance but is best made only a few hours before serving.

*Whisk the heated milk gradually into the yolk mixture.*

*Stir until the mixture thickens and will coat the back of a wooden spoon.*

Use a metal spoon to fold in the sifted combined flours a third at a time.

With a 1 cm nozzle, pipe the mixture in a close snaking pattern.

Trim the long side and ends of the sponge and wrap around the cheesecake.

## ORANGE AND PISTACHIO CHEESECAKE

Preparation time: 1 hour + overnight
 chilling
Total cooking time: Nil
Serves 8–10

200 g orange cream
 biscuits, crushed
75 g unsalted butter, melted
2/3 cup finely chopped
 pistachio nuts
1/4 cup orange marmalade
250 g cream cheese, softened
1 tablespoon grated orange rind
1/3 cup caster sugar
2 tablespoons honey
2/3 cup plain yoghurt

1/2 cup fresh orange juice
1 tablespoon gelatine
1 1/4 cups thickened cream,
 whipped to soft peaks
1 orange
whipped cream and chopped
 pistachio nuts, to decorate

**1** Lightly grease the base and side of a 23 cm round springform tin and line with non-stick baking paper. Combine the biscuit crumbs and butter, mix well and press into the base of the tin. Lightly roughen with a fork and refrigerate for 30 minutes. Combine the nuts and marmalade, spread over the biscuit base and chill.

**2** Beat the cream cheese, orange rind, sugar and honey until creamy. Add the yoghurt and juice, beating until well combined. Sprinkle the gelatine over 2 tablespoons water in a small bowl. Stand this over a larger bowl of hot water, stirring until the gelatine dissolves. Pour into the cream cheese mixture while beating. Gently fold in the cream. Pour into the tin and chill overnight, or until set.

**3** Cut a slice off each end of the orange and then cut away the skin in one spiral, removing all the pith. Separate the segments. Remove the cheesecake from the tin, press pistachio nuts around the side and top with cream, orange segments and nuts.

### COOK'S FILE

**Variation:** Use chopped roasted hazelnuts or almonds instead of the pistachio nuts.

*Spread the combined nuts and marmalade over the biscuit base, then refrigerate.*

*Pour the dissolved gelatine into the cream cheese mixture while beating.*

*Divide the orange into segments by removing all the white pith.*

*Brush the tin with oil or melted butter and line with non-stick paper.*

*Add the egg yolks and orange rind and beat until combined.*

*Stir in the glacé fruit, peel and chocolate until well mixed.*

*Bake for 50 minutes, or until the top of the cheesecake is golden.*

## SICILIAN RICOTTA CHEESECAKE

Preparation time: 35 minutes +
  6 hours chilling
Total cooking time: 50 minutes
Serves 10–12

250 g plain chocolate biscuits
125 g butter, melted
500 g ricotta cheese
250 g cream cheese, softened
1/2 cup caster sugar
3 egg yolks
2 teaspoons finely grated
  orange rind
180 g mixed glacé fruit,
  chopped
1/3 cup mixed peel
1/2 cup finely chopped chocolate
icing sugar, to dust

**1** Brush a 25 cm round springform tin with melted butter or oil and line the base and side with non-stick baking paper. Process the biscuits in a food processor for 20 seconds until finely crushed. Stir in the butter and mix until well combined. Spoon into the tin, pressing evenly and firmly over the base, and then refrigerate. Preheat the oven to 180°C.
**2** Beat the ricotta, cream cheese and caster sugar for 3 minutes, or until smooth. Beat in the yolks and rind.
**3** Stir in the glacé fruit, peel and chocolate until well mixed. Spoon evenly over the crust and smooth.
**4** Bake for 50 minutes, or until the top is golden brown and the filling almost firm. Cool in the tin, then cover and refrigerate for at least 6 hours. Remove from the tin and dust with sifted icing sugar.

### COOK'S FILE

**Storage time:** Will keep, covered and refrigerated, for up to three days but is unsuitable to freeze.

Pour the melted butter into the biscuit crumbs and process until well combined.

Gradually add the mashed banana, spices, orange rind, juice and rum.

Add the beaten egg gradually, beating well after each addition.

Pour the banana filling mixture over the biscuit base.

## BANANA RUM CHEESECAKE

Preparation time: 40 minutes +
  6 hours chilling
Total cooking time: 1 hour + cooling
Serves 6–8

185 g butternut biscuits
2 teaspoons ground ginger
75 g butter, melted
750 g cream cheese, softened
1/2 cup caster sugar
1 cup mashed banana
1/2 teaspoon ground cinnamon
1 teaspoon ground nutmeg
1 tablespoon grated orange rind
2 tablespoons orange juice
1/4 cup rum
4 eggs, lightly beaten
1/2 cup apricot jam
3 bananas, for topping

**1** Brush a 23 cm round springform tin with melted butter or oil and line the base with non-stick baking paper. Preheat the oven to 150°C. Put the biscuits and ground ginger in a food processor and process for 20 seconds, until finely crushed. Pour in the butter and process until well combined. Spoon into the tin and press evenly and firmly over the base. Refrigerate while you prepare the filling.

**2** Beat the cream cheese and sugar with electric beaters for 3 minutes, or until soft and smooth. Gradually add the banana, spices, orange rind, juice and rum and beat until well mixed.

**3** Add the egg gradually, beating well after each addition, until creamy. Pour into the tin and bake for 1 hour, then turn off the oven, leaving the door slightly ajar. Use a wooden spoon to hold the door open and leave the cheesecake for a further hour. Remove from the oven and cool completely. Chill for at least 6 hours.

**4** Heat the jam gently in a small pan, then sieve and leave to cool. Gently release the cheesecake from the tin. Cut the bananas into even slices and arrange over the cake. Carefully brush the banana with the jam and refrigerate until ready to serve.

### COOK'S FILE

**Note:** Slice and mash the bananas only when you are ready to use them. If left, they will discolour.

## BAKED LIME AND PASSIONFRUIT CHEESECAKE

Preparation time: 1 hour + overnight chilling
Total cooking time: 50–55 minutes
Serves 6–8

250 g sweet biscuits, crushed
125 g unsalted butter, melted
500 g cream cheese, softened
1/3 cup caster sugar
3 teaspoons grated lime rind
2 tablespoons fresh lime juice
2 eggs, lightly beaten
1/2 cup fresh passionfruit pulp

*Passionfruit Topping*
1 tablespoon caster sugar
3 teaspoons cornflour
1/2 cup fresh passionfruit pulp

**1** Lightly grease the base and side of a 20 cm round springform tin and line with non-stick baking paper. Preheat the oven to 160°C. Mix together the biscuit crumbs and butter. Press into the base and sides of the tin and chill for 30 minutes.

**2** Using electric beaters, beat the cream cheese, sugar, lime rind and juice until creamy. Gradually beat in the eggs and passionfruit pulp. Pour into the tin, put on a baking tray to catch any drips and bake for 45–50 minutes, or until just set. Remove from the oven and cool completely.

**3 To make the Topping:** Combine the sugar, cornflour and 2 tablespoons water in a small pan over low heat. Stir until smooth, add 2 more tablespoons water and the passionfruit pulp and stir until the mixture boils and thickens. Pour the hot topping over the cheesecake, spread evenly and then leave to cool completely. Refrigerate overnight.

### COOK'S FILE

**Hints:** You will need about eight fresh passionfruit for this recipe.
• Cream cheese is easier to beat if it is softened to room temperature.

*Use your fingertips to press the crumb mixture into the base and side of the tin.*

*Gradually beat in the eggs and passionfruit pulp.*

*Stir the Passionfruit Topping mixture until it boils and thickens.*

## APRICOT COINTREAU CHEESECAKE

Preparation time: 45 minutes +
  overnight chilling
Total cooking time: about 1 hour
Serves 6–8

200 g dried apricots
1 tablespoon soft brown sugar
2 tablespoons Cointreau
250 g sweet plain biscuits,
  finely crushed
1/2 teaspoon each of ground
  ginger, cinnamon and nutmeg
125 g butter, melted
375 g cream cheese, softened
1/3 cup caster sugar
2 teaspoons vanilla essence
4 eggs
1/2 cup thickened cream

*Topping*
300 g carton sour cream
1 tablespoon soft brown sugar
1 tablespoon Cointreau

**1** Put the apricots, brown sugar, Cointreau and 2 tablespoons water in a pan and stir gently over low heat until the sugar has dissolved. Cover and simmer for 5–10 minutes, or until the liquid is absorbed and the apricots soft and plump. Don't allow to burn. Remove from the heat and cool a little. Process until almost smooth.

**2** Brush a 20 cm round springform tin with melted butter or oil and line the base with non-stick baking paper. Mix together the crushed biscuits, spices and butter. Press half firmly into the base of the tin and gradually press the rest around the side. Use a glass to help press down the crust. Refrigerate for 10–15 minutes.

**3** Preheat the oven to 180°C. Beat together the cream cheese and sugar until smooth. Add the processed apricot and vanilla essence and beat well. Add the eggs one at a time, beating well after each addition. Beat in the cream and pour into the crust in the tin. Put on an oven tray to collect any drips and bake for 35 minutes.

**4 To make the Topping:** Stir together the sour cream, sugar and Cointreau until smooth. Carefully spread over the hot cheesecake, then return to the oven and bake for a further 10–15 minutes. Allow to cool completely then refrigerate overnight.

### COOK'S FILE

**Variation:** Dried peaches, prunes or pears can be used instead of apricots.

*Simmer the apricots until the liquid is absorbed and they are plump and soft.*

*Add the processed apricot and vanilla essence and beat well.*

*Use a spoon to carefully spread the topping over the hot cheesecake.*

## SULTANA CHEESECAKE SLICE

Preparation time: 1 hour
Total cooking time: 45 minutes
Serves 8–10

1½ cups plain flour
2 tablespoons icing sugar
½ cup custard powder
½ teaspoon baking powder
125 g butter, chopped
2–3 tablespoons milk

*Filling*
250 g light cream cheese
250 g cream cheese, softened
55 g butter
¼ cup sugar
2 eggs
1 tablespoon lemon juice
2 teaspoons finely grated
   lemon rind
¾ cup sultanas

**1** Preheat the oven to 180°C. Brush a 28 x 18 cm tin with melted butter or oil and line the base with non-stick baking paper. Sift the flour, sugar, custard and baking powders into a bowl, add the butter and rub with your fingertips until crumbly. Stir in enough milk to form a soft dough.
**2** Roll two-thirds of the pastry between 2 sheets of baking paper to make a rectangle large enough to line the base and sides of the tin. Trim the pastry edges and prick the pastry base randomly with a fork, then bake for 10 minutes. Allow to cool a little.
**3 To make the Filling:** Beat together the cream cheeses, butter and sugar until smooth. Beat in the eggs, juice and rind until combined. Stir in the sultanas. Pour into the tin. Roll the remaining pastry into a long rectangle, then cut into long thin strips. Lay the strips in a lattice pattern over the cheesecake, gently press to the edge of the pastry shell and trim. Bake for 30–35 minutes, or until set but not coloured. When cold, cut into pieces to serve.

*Rub the mixture together with your fingertips until fine and crumbly.*

*Trim the edges of the pastry with a sharp knife.*

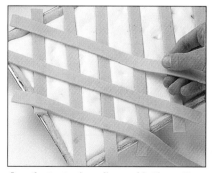

*Lay the pastry in a diagonal lattice pattern over the cheesecake.*

29

## CITRUS CHEESECAKE

Preparation time: 50 minutes
Total cooking time: 50–55 minutes +
 overnight chilling
Serves 6–8

250 g butter shortbread
 biscuits, finely crushed
1/2 teaspoon ground nutmeg
1/2 teaspoon ground cinnamon
100 g butter, melted

*Filling*
500 g cream cheese, softened
1/2 cup caster sugar
1 teaspoon vanilla essence
2 tablespoons citrus juice
2 tablespoons finely grated
 citrus rind (see note)
4 eggs, lightly beaten

*Topping*
300 g carton sour cream
1 teaspoon vanilla essence
1 tablespoon demerara sugar
1 tablespoon citrus juice

**1** Brush a 20 cm round springform
tin with melted butter or oil and line
the base with non-stick baking paper.
Mix together the biscuits, spices and
butter in a bowl until moistened.
**2** Press half the mixture firmly into
the tin base and gradually press the
rest around the side to a little below
the top edge. Refrigerate for 10–15
minutes. Preheat the oven to 180°C.
**3** Beat the cream cheese and sugar
with electric beaters until smooth and
creamy. Add the vanilla essence, juice
and rind and beat until combined.
Add the eggs gradually, beating well
after each addition. Pour into the tin
and put on a baking tray to catch any
drips. Bake for 40 minutes.
**4** Mix together the topping ingredients and pour over the hot cheesecake;
smooth the surface. Bake for a further
10 minutes, then cool completely and
refrigerate overnight. Try serving
topped with freshly whipped cream
and candied citrus rind.

### COOK'S FILE

**Note:** For the citrus rind and juice
choose from lemon, lime, orange,
mandarin, grapefruit or tangelo or use
a combination.

*Grate the rind of the citrus fruits finely,
avoiding the pith.*

*Firmly press half the mixture into the tin
base, using the back of a spoon.*

*Add the vanilla essence, juice, rind and
eggs; beat until combined.*

*Mix together the topping ingredients in a
large bowl.*

## HONEY CINNAMON CHEESECAKE WITH PRALINE CRUST

Preparation time: 1 hour + freezing
Total cooking time: 25 minutes
Serves 8–10

100 g flaked almonds
3/4 cup sugar
200 g plain sweet biscuits
100 g unsalted butter, melted
250 g mascarpone cheese
250 g cream cheese, softened
400 g can condensed milk
1/4 cup honey
300 ml cream
2 teaspoons ground cinnamon

**1** Preheat the oven to 150°C. To make the praline, spread the almonds on a foil-lined, greased baking tray. Put the sugar in a pan with 1/2 cup water and stir over low heat until the sugar has dissolved. Bring to the boil, then simmer without stirring until the toffee is golden brown. Pour over the almonds, then set aside to cool and harden before breaking into pieces.

**2** Brush a 22.5 or 23 cm round spring-form tin with melted butter or oil and line the base with non-stick baking paper. Reserve about half the praline and process the rest with the biscuits, until finely chopped. Stir in the butter and press into the base and side of the tin. Bake for 15 minutes and then leave to cool.

**3** Process the mascarpone and cream cheese together until soft and creamy. Add the condensed milk and honey. Whip the cream until soft peaks form and then fold in. Pour into the tin, sprinkle with cinnamon and swirl gently with a skewer. Do not overmix. Put in the freezer for several hours, or until firm, and serve decorated with the remaining pieces of praline. Delicious with poached cinnamon pears or dried fruit compote.

### COOK'S FILE

**Storage time:** Can be frozen for up to one week.

**Hint:** It is always easiest to soften cream cheese to room temperature before trying to beat it.

*Pour the toffee over the flaked almonds on the tray.*

*Process the praline with the biscuits until finely crushed.*

*Use a skewer to swirl the cinnamon through the cheesecake filling.*

## CHOCOLATE COLLAR CHEESECAKE

Preparation time: 1½ hours + chilling
Total cooking time: 50 minutes
Serves 8–10

200 g chocolate cream biscuits,
    finely crushed
70 g butter, melted

*Filling*
250 g light cream cheese, at
    room temperature
250 g cream cheese, at room
    temperature
⅓ cup sugar
2 eggs
1 tablespoon dark cocoa powder
300 g carton sour cream
250 g dark chocolate, melted
⅓ cup Bailey's Irish Cream
50 g white chocolate
    melts, melted
150 g dark chocolate, extra,
    melted
1¼ cups thickened cream
dark cocoa powder and icing
    sugar, for dusting

**1** Brush a 23 cm round springform tin with melted butter or oil and line the base and side with non-stick baking paper. Mix together the biscuit crumbs and butter until all the crumbs are moistened. Press the mixture firmly into the base of the tin and refrigerate for 10 minutes. Preheat the oven to moderate 180°C.

**2 To make the Filling:** Beat the cream cheeses and sugar with electric beaters until smooth and creamy. Add the eggs, one at a time, beating well after each addition. Beat in the cocoa powder and sour cream until smooth.

Add the cooled melted dark chocolate and continue beating until smooth. Beat in the liqueur and pour over the crumb base, smooth the surface and bake for 45 minutes. The cheesecake may not be fully set at this stage, but will firm up when left to stand. Allow to cool and refrigerate, overnight if possible, until completely cold.

**3** Carefully remove the cheesecake from the tin and put on a board.

**4** Measure the height of the cheesecake with a ruler and add 5 mm. Cut a strip of non-stick baking paper this wide and 75 cm long. Pipe or drizzle the cooled, melted white chocolate in a figure eight pattern along the paper.

**5** Allow the white chocolate to just set, then spread the extra melted dark chocolate in a layer over the entire strip of paper. Allow the chocolate to set a little, but you need to be able to bend the paper without it cracking.

**6** Working quickly, wrap the paper around the cheesecake with the chocolate on the inside. Seal the ends and hold the paper in place until the chocolate sets completely. Carefully peel away the paper to leave the chocolate around the side of the cheesecake. Whip the cream to firm peaks. Spread the cream on top of the cheesecake and dust very generously with cocoa powder or a mixture or cocoa powder and icing sugar.

### COOK'S FILE

**Note:** The chocolate collar can be made in any pattern you like—try piping white circles or spots. If you are limited for time, this deliciously rich cheesecake can be made without the chocolate collar.

**Hint:** It's best not to attempt the chocolate collar on a very hot day—the chocolate will be too soft to handle.

*Press the chocolate biscuit crumb base firmly into the tin.*

*Add the cooled melted chocolate and beat until smooth.*

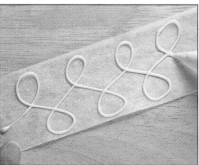

*Pipe the white chocolate in a pattern along the paper.*

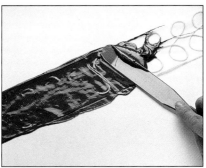

*Allow the white chocolate to just set, then spread the paper with dark chocolate.*

*Working quickly, wrap the paper around the cake, chocolate on the inside.*

*Carefully peel away the paper to leave the chocolate around the cheesecake.*

# CREAMY MASCARPONE AND PRUNE CHEESECAKE

Preparation time: 1 hour 20 minutes + overnight chilling
Total cooking time: 1 hour 20 minutes
Serves 8–10

200 g pitted prunes
1/3 cup brandy
2 tablespoons and 1/2 cup caster sugar
250 g plain chocolate biscuits
50 g almond meal

100 g melted butter
500 g mascarpone cheese
250 g cream cheese, softened
2 eggs
300 g sour cream

**1** Put the prunes, brandy and the 2 tablespoons sugar in a bowl and leave for 1 hour. Brush a 23 cm springform tin with melted butter and line with non-stick baking paper. Dust with flour. Preheat the oven to 150°C.
**2** Simmer the prunes and brandy in a pan over low heat for 10 minutes until the prunes have swelled. Remove from the heat and leave to cool. Process

together the biscuits and almond meal until crumbly; mix in the butter. Press into the base and side of the tin. Refrigerate for 10 minutes.
**3** Process the mascarpone, cream cheese and remaining sugar until smooth. Add the eggs and sour cream and process. Layer the prunes over the crust and pour the mascarpone filling over the top. Bake for 1 hour 10 minutes, or until set. Cool to room temperature and refrigerate overnight.

### COOK'S FILE

**Note:** This is well suited to a topping of whipped cream and plum slices.

*Sprinkle the tin with flour and shake off any excess.*

*Simmer the prunes over low heat until they have swelled.*

*Pour the mascarpone filling over the prunes in the crumb crust.*

Use a glass to press half the mixture into the base and the rest around the side.

Pour the filling mixture into the biscuit base in the tin.

Heat the butter, sugar, jam and brandy in a large non-stick pan and stir.

If you only have a small pan, cook the apple in batches until tender but still firm.

## GOLDEN APPLE CHEESECAKE

Preparation time: 55 minutes + chilling
Total cooking time: 1 hour 10 minutes
Serves 6–8

250 g granita and fruit biscuits
1/2 teaspoon ground cardamom
100 g butter, melted
375 g cream cheese, softened
1/2 cup soft brown sugar
1/4 cup condensed milk
1/2 cup sour cream
2 teaspoons vanilla essence
1 tablespoon custard powder
4 eggs

*Topping*
30 g butter
1/4 cup sugar
2 tablespoons apricot jam
1 tablespoon brandy
2 red apples (Royal Gala or
   Pink Lady), unpeeled, cored
   and thinly sliced

**1** Brush a 20 cm round springform tin with melted butter or oil and line the base with non-stick baking paper. Finely crush the biscuits, then put in a bowl with the cardamom and butter, stirring until all the crumbs are moistened. Press half the mixture firmly into the base of the tin and the remainder around the side, but not quite up to the top edge of the tin. Refrigerate for 10–15 minutes.

**2** Preheat the oven to 180°C. Beat the cream cheese and sugar until smooth and creamy. Add the condensed milk, sour cream, vanilla essence and custard powder and beat well. Add the eggs one at a time, beating well. Pour into the tin and put on a baking tray to catch any excess butter that may ooze out. Bake for 40 minutes.

**3** **To make the Topping:** Heat the butter, sugar, jam and brandy in a large non-stick frying pan and stir over medium heat until the sugar is dissolved. Simmer gently for 1 minute. Add the apple slices in a single layer; simmer for 3–5 minutes or until tender but still firm. Cool in the syrup.

**4** Lay overlapping slices of apple around the edge of the cheesecake and a few in the middle. Bake for a further 15–20 minutes. Simmer the remaining apple syrup for 2–3 minutes, brush over the warm cheesecake, then allow to cool completely. Chill for several hours in the tin before serving.

# PAVLOVAS

## FRESH FRUIT PAVLOVA

Preparation time: 30 minutes
Total cooking time: 40–45 minutes
Serves 6–8

4 egg whites
1 cup caster sugar
1¹/2 cups cream, whipped
1 banana, sliced
250 g punnet strawberries,
    sliced
2 kiwi fruit, sliced
pulp from 2 passionfruit

**1** Preheat the oven to slow 150°C. Line a large oven tray with non-stick baking paper and draw a 20 cm circle on the paper. Beat the egg whites with electric beaters in a large dry bowl until soft peaks form. Gradually add the sugar, beating well after each addition. Beat for 5–10 minutes until all the sugar has completely dissolved.
**2** Spread the meringue mixture onto the tray inside the marked circle. Shape the meringue evenly, running the flat side of a palette knife along the edge and over the top.
**3** Run the palette knife up the edge of meringue mixture, all the way round, making furrows. This strengthens the pavlova, stops the edge crumbling and gives it a good, decorative finish.
**4** Bake for 30 minutes, or until pale and crisp. Reduce the heat to 120°C and bake for a further 10–15 minutes. Turn off the oven and leave the pavlova inside to cool, using a wooden spoon to keep the door ajar. Top with whipped cream and arrange with fruit. Drizzle with passionfruit pulp.

### COOK'S FILE

**Storage time:** Pavlova is best eaten on the day it is made. Top with cream and fruit just before serving.

*Gradually add the sugar, beating well after each addition.*

*Spread the meringue mixture inside the marked circle.*

*Run a flat-bladed knife up the edge of the meringue to make furrows.*

*Then run the knife back down again so the furrows are neat.*

## APRICOT DACQUOISE

Preparation time: 1 hour + cooling
Total cooking time: 1 hour
Serves 6–8

1 cup slivered almonds
4 egg whites
pinch of cream of tartar
1 cup plus 1–2 tablespoons
   caster sugar
200 g dried apricots
1 teaspoon lemon juice
100 g white chocolate
1¼ cups thickened cream
1 tablespoon icing sugar
1 teaspoon vanilla essence

**1** Preheat the oven to 160°C. Put the almonds on a baking tray and toast for 8 minutes or until lightly browned. Leave to cool. Line 2 oven trays with non-stick baking paper and draw one 18 cm circle in the middle of each. Put the egg whites and cream of tartar in a dry bowl and beat until firm peaks form. Gradually add 1 cup caster sugar, beating hard until thick and glossy. Fold through the toasted almonds and spread evenly onto the circles, piling the mixture into rough mounds. Bake for 40 minutes, or until crisp, and then turn off the oven and cool the meringues with the door ajar.
**2** Put the apricots in a small pan and cover with warm water; soak for at least 1 hour. Simmer for 10 minutes, or until the apricots are tender. Drain and cool. Purée in a food processor, adding 1–2 tablespoons caster sugar, to taste, and the lemon juice. Melt the chocolate in a bowl over simmering water. Spread thinly onto a smooth flat surface, preferably marble. When just set, use a sharp knife to scrape

thin layers of chocolate curls. Store in a single layer until needed.
**3** Beat the cream, icing sugar and vanilla essence, until firm peaks form. Fold in the apricot purée, allowing the apricot to streak the cream. Peel the paper from the meringues, put one meringue top side down on a serving plate and spread with half the cream. Sandwich with the other meringue,

crisp side up, and top with the remaining cream. Chill for 1 hour before serving. Top with chocolate curls and dust with icing sugar.

**C O O K ' S   F I L E**

**Storage time:** Meringue may be made several hours in advance. If filled with cream, it will soften and be easier to slice.

*Pile the meringue mixture into rough mounds in the circles.*

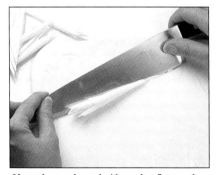

*Use a large sharp knife and a flat surface to make chocolate curls.*

*Gently fold in the apricot purée, allowing it to streak the cream.*

*Gently fold in the ground pecans, until just mixed.*

*Drizzle melted chocolate over the whole pecans on the paper-lined tray.*

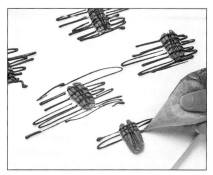

*Spread half the chocolate over the meringue with a palette knife.*

*Spread cream around the side of the meringue with a palette knife.*

## RASPBERRY PECAN TORTE

Preparation time: 1 hour
Total cooking time: 50 minutes
Serves 6–8

4 egg whites
1¼ cups caster sugar
1 teaspoon vinegar
½ teaspoon vanilla essence
70 g ground pecans
50 g dark compound chocolate
12 whole roasted pecans
150 g dark chocolate, chopped
1½ cups cream, whipped to
   firm peaks
350 g fresh raspberries
icing sugar, to dust

**1** Preheat the oven to 180°C. Line the bases of two 20 cm springform tins with non-stick baking paper. Put the egg whites in a large dry bowl and beat to soft peaks. Gradually add the caster sugar, a tablespoon at a time, beating well after each addition. Beat for 8–10 minutes, or until the sugar is dissolved. Beat in the vinegar and vanilla essence. Gently fold in the ground pecans, until just mixed. Spread evenly into the tins and smooth. Bake for 40–45 minutes, or until crisp, then leave to cool in the oven with the door ajar. Remove from the tins, leaving the baking paper on.
**2** Melt the compound chocolate in a heatproof bowl over a pan of gently simmering water. Put the whole pecans on a tray lined with baking paper and drizzle with chocolate. Allow to set. Peel away the paper.
**3** Melt the remaining chocolate. Put a meringue, crisp side down, on a plate and remove the baking paper. Spread half the chocolate over the meringue with a palette knife and then spread ½ cup cream over the chocolate. Arrange two-thirds of the raspberries over the cream.
**4** Remove the paper from the second meringue, spread the underside with the remaining chocolate and put on top of the first, chocolate side down. Spread another ½ cup cream around the side of meringue. Top with the remaining cream, pecans and berries.

### COOK'S FILE

**Storage time:** Meringue may be made several hours ahead but should be assembled just before serving.

## BLUEBERRY MERINGUE CAKE

Preparation time: 35 minutes
Total cooking time: about 2 hours
Serves 6–8

340 g packet butter cake mix
2 tablespoons grated
    orange rind
250 g fresh blueberries
plain flour, to dust
4 egg whites

¼ teaspoon cream of tartar
1 cup caster sugar

**1** Preheat the oven to 150°C. Grease a 22.5 or 23 cm round springform tin and line with non-stick baking paper to extend about 5 cm above the rim. Prepare the cake mix as directed on the packet. Beat in the rind. Spoon the mixture into the tin and smooth the surface. Dust the blueberries with flour and shake off the excess. Drop them onto the cake mixture.
**2** Beat together the egg whites, cream of tartar and caster sugar until thick and dissolved (about 5 minutes). Spoon over the cake mix and spread evenly, swirling the meringue. Bake for 1 hour 50 minutes to 2 hours, until the meringue is crisp and a skewer comes out clean when inserted.
**3** Allow the cake to rest in the tin for 15 minutes before easing out. Serve warm with whipped cream.

### COOK'S FILE

**Note:** Frozen or well-drained tinned blueberries can be used instead.

*Dust the blueberries with a little flour and drop onto the cake mixture.*

*Beat the meringue mixture until thick, glossy and stiff.*

*Carefully swirl the meringue mixture over the cake mix.*

*Sprinkle the flaked almonds over the uncooked meringue.*

*Turn out the meringue onto baking paper sprinkled with sugar and cinnamon.*

*Use a metal spoon to gently fold in the chopped strawberries.*

*Use the baking paper to help you roll the meringue from the long side.*

## STRAWBERRY PASSIONFUIT PAVLOVA ROLL

Preparation time: 40 minutes
Total cooking time: 10 minutes
Serves 6–8

4 egg whites
3/4 cup caster sugar
1/3 cup flaked almonds
1 teaspoon ground cinnamon

*Cream Filling*
250 g fresh strawberries
1 cup thickened cream, chilled
1/4 cup strawberry liqueur
pulp of 2 passionfruit

**1** Preheat the oven to 180°C. Lightly grease a 30 x 25 cm swiss roll tin with melted butter and line the base and sides with non-stick baking paper. Grease lightly with melted butter. Beat the egg whites in a large dry bowl with electric beaters, until soft peaks form. Gradually beat in almost all the sugar, leaving about 1 table-spoon, and beat for 5 minutes. Spread the meringue evenly into the tin and smooth. Sprinkle with flaked almonds.
**2** Bake for 10 minutes, or until firm to touch. Put a large sheet of baking paper on a work surface and sprinkle with the reserved caster sugar and the cinnamon. Turn the meringue out onto this, peel off the lining paper and cool for 2 minutes.
**3 To make the Cream Filling:** Reserve a few whole strawberries for decoration. Chop the rest finely, being careful not to mash. Beat the cream into soft peaks, then mix in the liqueur gradually. Fold in the chopped strawberries and spread over the slightly warm meringue. Spoon the passionfruit pulp over the cream.
**4** Use the baking paper to help you roll the meringue firmly from the long side, ending with the seam under-neath. Cover with plastic wrap and refrigerate until cold. Trim the ends with a sharp knife before serving.

### COOK'S FILE

**Notes:** The meringue needs to be lukewarm for rolling, otherwise it will crack. Serve within 3–4 hours as meringue weeps if left filled any longer. Unsuitable to freeze. Delicious with a sauce of puréed strawberries.

## FROZEN PRALINE MERINGUE TORTE

Preparation time: 1 hour + freezing
Total cooking time: 1 hour 10 minutes
Serves 8–10

4 egg whites
1¹/2 cups caster sugar
100 g blanched almonds
2 litre carton good quality
    vanilla ice cream, softened

*Strawberry Sauce*
500 g fresh strawberries
2 tablespoons lemon juice
¹/4 cup icing sugar

**1** Preheat the oven to 150°C and line 2 baking trays with non-stick baking paper. Use a 20 cm tin as a guide to draw 2 circles on the paper. Brush with oil and dust with a little caster sugar. Beat the egg whites to stiff peaks and then gradually add 1 cup of the sugar (about 1 tablespoon at a time). Beat until the mixture is thick and glossy and the sugar dissolved. Pipe meringue into the 2 circles. Bake for 1 hour and then cool in the oven.

**2** To make praline, line a baking tray with non-stick baking paper and sprinkle with almonds. Put the remaining ¹/2 cup sugar with ¹/3 cup water in a pan and stir over low heat until dissolved. Bring to the boil without stirring and, when golden, pour over the almonds. Allow to set and cool before grinding finely in a food processor or with a rolling pin.

**3** Process or beat the ice cream until creamy and fold in the praline. Put a meringue circle into a lined 22 cm springform tin, spoon in the ice cream and put the other meringue on top.

Keep in the freezer until ready to serve with Strawberry Sauce.

**4 To make Strawberry Sauce:** Process all the ingredients until smooth. Add a little water if too thick.

**Storage time:** Torte will keep for up to four days in the freezer.
**Note:** Meringues should be cooked very slowly to be dry and crunchy.

*Pipe meringue into the two circles on the baking trays.*

*When the syrup turns golden, pour it over the almonds.*

*Spoon the ice cream into the tin, on top of the first meringue.*

## FLUFFY PAVLOVA

Preparation time: 40 minutes + cooling
Total cooking time: 50–55 minutes
Serves 4–6

5 egg whites
1 cup sugar
2 teaspoons white vinegar
2 teaspoons cornflour
small pinch of baking powder
1¹/4 cups cream
cherries, pears, nectarines or
      other fresh fruit, to decorate

**1** Preheat the oven to 150°C and brush a 20 cm round springform tin with melted butter or oil. Line the base and side with non-stick baking paper, extending 3 cm above the rim. Grease the paper and dust the base and side with cornflour, shaking off any excess.

**2** Beat the egg whites in a large dry bowl with electric beaters until soft peaks form. Add the sugar gradually, beating well after each addition until thick and glossy and the sugar has dissolved. Beat in the vinegar, cornflour and baking powder. Spoon into

the tin and smooth the surface. Bake for 50–55 minutes, or until well risen and lightly browned on the surface. Turn the oven off but leave the meringue inside until completely cool.

**3** Whip the cream until soft peaks form and spread over the pavlova. Arrange the slices of fruit decoratively on top and serve immediately.

### COOK'S FILE

**Note:** Best eaten the same day. Top with cream and fruit just before serving to prevent weeping. The crunchy edge will collapse a little on standing.

*Lightly greasing the tin before lining it helps the paper to stay in place.*

*Beat the cornflour, vinegar and baking powder into the egg white mixture.*

*Whip the cream until soft peaks form and then spread over the pavlova.*

# Meringues

Crunchy meringues are a delicious contrast when served with soft mousses or custards. They are quick and simple to make and, piped into elegant shapes, can even be served as accompaniments to after-dinner coffee.

## BASIC MERINGUE RECIPE

Preheat the oven to 150°C. Beat 2 egg whites into stiff peaks with electric beaters. Gradually add ½ cup caster sugar, beating well after each addition. Continue beating until thick and glossy and the sugar is dissolved. Spoon into a piping bag and pipe into small shapes on baking trays lined with non-stick baking paper. Bake for 20–25 minutes, or until just crisp. Turn off the oven, leaving the meringues inside with the door ajar to cool. Makes about 30.

### Chocolate Meringue Fingers

Prepare the basic recipe until the mixture is thick and glossy and then beat in 1 tablespoon sifted cocoa powder. Spoon into a piping bag fitted with a plain round nozzle. Pipe fine 8 cm lengths onto the prepared trays, allowing room for them to spread. Bake as above and serve drizzled with melted chocolate or dusted with dark cocoa powder combined with a little icing sugar. Makes about 40.

### Custard Discs

Prepare the basic recipe until the mixture is thick and glossy. Beat in 1 tablespoon custard powder and spoon into a piping bag fitted with a plain 5 mm or 1 cm round nozzle. Pipe spiral discs onto the trays. Bake as above. Serve dusted with icing sugar or drizzled with melted chocolate. Makes about 40.

### Coffee Kisses

Prepare the basic recipe until the mixture is thick and glossy. Beat in 2–3 teaspoons instant coffee powder. Spoon into a piping bag fitted with a small star nozzle and pipe into small stars on the trays. Bake as above. The meringues can be sandwiched together with 60 g melted white or dark chocolate or served plain. Makes about 30.

### Hazelnut Snails

Prepare the basic recipe until the mixture is thick and glossy. Beat in 2 tablespoons ground hazelnuts and spoon into a piping bag fitted with a plain 1 cm nozzle. Pipe in fine zig-zag lengths onto the trays and bake as above. Serve dusted with a mixture of icing sugar and ground cinnamon or drizzled with melted chocolate. Makes 30.

### Meringue Nests

Prepare the basic recipe until thick and glossy. Spoon into a piping bag fitted with a small star nozzle and pipe into nests on the trays. Bake as above. Serve filled with whipped cream flavoured with coffee or chocolate liqueur topped with a chocolate-coated coffee bean, or fill the centre with a chocolate truffle mixture and top with a slice of strawberry. Makes about 40.

*Clockwise from top left: Basic Meringues;*
*Coffee Kisses; Hazelnut Snails; Meringue Nests;*
*Custard Discs; Chocolate Meringue Fingers*

## BERRY NESTS

Preparation time: 30 minutes + cooling
Total cooking time: 1 hour 15 minutes
Makes 12

4 egg whites
small pinch of cream of tartar
1 cup caster sugar
1¼ cups thickened cream
2 teaspoons icing sugar
1 tablespoon brandy
fresh mixed berries

**1** Line a large baking tray with non-stick baking paper and preheat the oven to 150°C. Beat the egg whites and cream of tartar until soft peaks form then gradually add the sugar. Beat until stiff and glossy.
**2** Fit a piping bag with a medium-sized star nozzle and use to pipe tightly coiled spirals of meringue (about 8 cm across) onto the prepared tray. Pipe rings on the top edges of the rounds to form nests.
**3** Bake for 30 minutes. Reduce the oven to 120°C and bake for a further 45 minutes. Turn the oven off and allow the nests to cool in the oven with the door ajar. Whip the cream with the icing sugar and brandy. Pile into the nests and top with mixed berries of your choice.

### COOK'S FILE

**Note:** The cream of tartar will help to dry the meringues, making them crisp and crunchy. Pavlova nests are also delicious served with a simple coulis of puréed fresh berries, perhaps sweetened with a little icing sugar.

*Beat the egg whites in a clean dry bowl until soft peaks form.*

*Pipe tightly coiled spirals of meringue to form nests.*

*Spoon the flavoured whipped cream into the nests and top with berries.*

*Pipe 5 cm round meringues onto the prepared tray.*

*Work the ground almonds roughly into the meringues with a fork or spatula.*

## STRAWBERRY CREAM MERINGUE GATEAU

Preparation time: 1½ hours + cooling
Total cooking time: 2 hours 10 minutes
Serves 8

8 egg whites
2 cups caster sugar
1 tablespoon cornflour
100 g ground almonds

*Strawberry Cream*
500 g fresh strawberries
1½ cups thickened cream
2 tablespoons strawberry
  liqueur
icing sugar, to dust

**1** Line a baking tray with non-stick baking paper and preheat the oven to 140°C. Beat 2 of the egg whites until firm peaks form. Add ½ cup sugar gradually, beating well after each addition. Beat for 5 minutes until stiff and glossy. Fit a large plain nozzle onto a large piping bag and pipe 5 cm round meringues onto the tray. Bake for 40 minutes. Turn off the oven and leave the meringues until cold.

**2** Line 2 baking trays with non-stick baking paper and draw a 25 cm circle on each. Beat the remaining egg whites until firm. Add the remaining sugar gradually, beating until stiff and glossy. Beat in the cornflour, then spoon or pipe into the circles and smooth. Work the ground almonds roughly into the meringues with a fork or spatula and bake at 150°C for 1½ hours. Leave to cool in the oven.

**3 To make Strawberry Cream:** Hull and slice half the strawberries. Beat the cream into soft peaks and add the liqueur gradually, beating into firm peaks. Gently fold in the sliced strawberries.

**4** Spread one large meringue with Strawberry Cream and put the other on top. Sandwich the small meringues to the top with a little cream. Spoon the remaining cream into the centre, top with strawberries and dust with icing sugar.

**COOK'S FILE**

**Storage time:** Small meringues may be stored in an airtight container in the refrigerator for up to two days.

*Gently fold the sliced strawberries into the liqueur-flavoured cream.*

*Spread one meringue with Strawberry Cream and then put the other on top.*

Make the large meringues on the day of serving. The cream can be kept in the fridge for several hours but serve the cake within 1 hour of assembling.

# BLACK FOREST PAVLOVA

Preparation time: 1 hour + soaking
Total cooking time: 1 hour 10 minutes
  + cooling
Serves 8–10

2 cups dark pitted sour or
    morello cherries, drained
1/4 cup cherry brandy
2 cinnamon sticks
6 whole cloves
a little cornflour, for dusting
6 egg whites
1 1/2 cups caster sugar
2 tablespoons cocoa powder
450 g dark chocolate, chopped
2 1/4 cups thickened or
    pouring cream
fresh cherries, for decoration

**1** Put the cherries, brandy, cinnamon sticks and cloves in a bowl, cover with plastic wrap and leave for several hours, or overnight.

**2** Preheat the oven to 150°C and line 3 baking trays with non-stick baking paper. Draw a 20 cm circle on each sheet and sprinkle lightly with cornflour. Beat the egg whites with electric beaters until stiff peaks form. Add the sugar gradually, beating well after each addition. Continue beating until thick and glossy and all the sugar is dissolved. Beat in the cocoa.

**3** Spread the meringue evenly over the circles on the trays. Bake for 1 hour, or until crisp, and then turn the oven off and leave the meringues inside until completely cool.

**4** Put 200 g chocolate and 1/4 cup cream in a small heatproof bowl and stand over a pan of simmering water. Stir until the chocolate has melted and the mixture is smooth. Allow to cool

slightly before spreading evenly over the three meringue discs, almost up to the edge.

**5** Beat the remaining cream until firm peaks form and then spread a third of it over one of the meringue discs. Top with half the drained cherries. Put a second meringue layer on top. Top with half the remaining cream and the rest of the cherries. Put the last meringue on top and spread with the rest of the cream.

**6** Melt the remaining chocolate and spread in a thin layer over a cool smooth surface (a marble board would be perfect but a formica work surface will suffice). Using the edge of a sharp knife at a 45° angle, scrape thin strips of chocolate (scrape away from your body to be safe). The strips will curl as they come away. If the chocolate breaks it has set too hard and needs to be re-melted. Decorate the pavlova with a heap of fresh cherries and chocolate curls.

### COOK'S FILE

**Storage time:** The meringue discs can be made a day in advance. Store in an airtight container but assemble the pavlova just prior to serving. The cherries can be left to soak for several days. Store, covered, in the fridge. The longer they soak, the better the flavour will be. Chocolate curls can be refrigerated between two sheets of greaseproof paper for up to 2 weeks, or frozen for up to 6 months.

**Variation:** Pitted fresh cherries can be used in this recipe. Add 2 tablespoons water and 1 tablespoon sugar to the brandy mixture and simmer the cherries over low heat for about 5 minutes instead of just leaving to macerate. Allow to cool and then drain before using.

*Put the cherries, brandy, cinnamon sticks and cloves in a bowl.*

*Draw a 20 cm diameter circle on the paper-lined baking trays.*

*Spread the meringue evenly into the circles, smoothing with a spatula.*

*Put some of the chocolate and cream into a small heatproof bowl to melt.*

*Spread the whipped cream over one of the meringue discs and top with cherries.*

*Shave off thick curls of dark chocolate with a sharp knife.*

## PAVLOVA ROLL WITH RASPBERRY COULIS

Preparation time: 30 minutes
Total cooking time: 12 minutes
Serves 8–10

4 egg whites
1 cup caster sugar
1 teaspoon cornflour
2 teaspoons lemon juice
    or vinegar
2/3 cup cream, whipped
1/4 cup chopped fresh berries

*Raspberry Coulis*
2 tablespoons brandy

250 g fresh raspberries
1 tablespoon icing sugar

**1** Brush a 25 x 30 cm swiss roll tin with oil and line with non-stick baking paper extending up 2 sides. Preheat the oven to 180°C. Beat the egg whites into soft peaks. Gradually add 1/2 cup plus 2 tablespoons of sugar and beat until thick and glossy. Combine 1 tablespoon of sugar with the cornflour. Fold into the meringue with the lemon juice or vinegar. Spoon into the tin and smooth. Bake for 12 minutes, until springy.
**2** Put a large sheet of baking paper on top of a clean tea towel on a work surface and sprinkle with the remain-

ing sugar. Turn the pavlova out onto this, peel off the paper and leave for 2 minutes. Roll up from the long side around the tea towel and allow to cool. Fold the berries into the cream.
**3** Unroll the pavlova, fill with the cream mixture and re-roll without the tea towel and baking paper. Transfer to a plate and serve, sliced, with Raspberry Coulis.
**4 To make Raspberry Coulis:** Put the brandy, raspberries and icing sugar in a food processor and process until well blended.

### COOK'S FILE

**Variation:** If preferred, a thick fruit purée can be used as a filling.

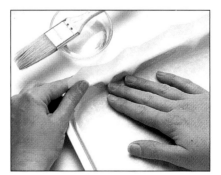

*Brushing the tin with oil before lining helps to keep the paper in place.*

*Roll the pavlova from the long side, around a tea towel.*

*Put the raspberries in a food processor with the brandy and sugar.*

## CHOCOLATE MERINGUE TOWER

Preparation time: 1–2 hour + cooling
Total cooking time: about 1 hour
Serves 8–10

8 egg whites
1 1/3 cups caster sugar
1/2 teaspoon vanilla essence
1/4 cup plain flour, sifted
250 g ground almonds
300 g dark chocolate, melted
2 1/2 cups cream, whipped
300 g milk chocolate, melted
50 g each extra dark and milk
    chocolate, to decorate

**1** Preheat the oven to 120°C. Beat the egg whites until stiff. Gradually beat in 2/3 cup sugar until the meringue is stiff and glossy. Beat in the vanilla essence. Mix together the remaining sugar, flour and ground almonds and gently fold into the meringue.

**2** Draw 4 circles on pieces of non-stick baking paper, each circle about 20 cm in diameter, and place on oven trays. Spread meringue evenly into each circle. Bake for 1 hour (you may have to make and cook the meringues in two batches). Cool completely and then peel off the paper.

**3** Spread the top of one meringue with a quarter of the melted dark chocolate and then a quarter of the whipped cream. Spread the underside of the remaining 3 meringues with the melted milk chocolate. Put one of these, milk chocolate side down, on top of the first meringue. Spread this with dark chocolate and cream and top with another meringue. Continue layering until all are used. Decorate with lattice chocolate (see page 5).

*Gently fold the mixture of sugar, flour and almonds into the meringue.*

*Spread the underside of three of the meringues with melted milk chocolate.*

*Sandwich together the meringues with a layer of dark chocolate and cream.*

# Parfaits and Biscuits

## WARM CARAMEL, NUT AND BANANA PARFAIT

Put 100 g butter, 1/2 cup soft brown sugar, 2 tablespoons golden syrup, 1/4 cup sour cream and 1 cup cream in a pan and whisk over low heat until all the sugar is dissolved. Simmer gently without stirring for 5 minutes (be careful it doesn't boil over) and remove from the heat. When the bubbles have subsided, stir in 1/2 cup condensed milk. Cool slightly. Layer sliced banana, scoops of vanilla ice cream, crushed pecans and warm caramel sauce in dessert glasses. (The sauce can be refrigerated in an airtight container.) Drizzle a little chocolate liqueur over the top of each parfait if you like. Serves 4–6.

## GOLDEN NUT CAKES

Combine 150 g ground pecans, walnuts or almonds, 1 1/4 cups plain flour, 1 1/4 teaspoons baking powder and 3/4 cup caster sugar in a large bowl. Make a well in the centre. Mix together 2/3 cup milk, 2 eggs, 2 tablespoons vegetable oil and 2 teaspoons vanilla essence and stir into the well. Add some grated orange or lemon rind at this point if you like. Stir until smooth and then spoon in tablespoons into greased shallow patty tins and bake in a preheated 180°C oven for 15–20 minutes, or until a skewer comes out clean when inserted in the centre. Transfer to a wire rack to cool while you cook the remaining mixture. Makes 34.

## RICH CHOCOLATE PARFAIT

Put 200 g chopped dark chocolate, 1/2 cup cream, 1/4 cup chocolate-based liqueur and 40 g butter in a pan. Stir over a low heat until smooth and allow to cool a little. Put a scoop each of three different ice creams (make at least one a chocolate flavour) into each dessert glass. Pour over the hot chocolate sauce and serve immediately. Serves 4–6.

## MANGO AND MACAROON PARFAIT

Put 3 small macaroons each into 4 parfait glasses. Spoon 1–2 teaspoons Grand Marnier or rum into each glass and sprinkle with icing sugar. Chill for 30 minutes. Peel and thinly slice 1 large or 2 small mangoes over the macaroons. Whip $1/2$ cup cream to soft peaks, then carefully fold in $1/3$ cup softened mascarpone cheese, $1/3$ cup custard and 1–2 teaspoons vanilla essence. Spoon into the glasses and top with scoops of vanilla and mango ice cream. Sprinkle with toasted flaked almonds before serving. Serves 4.

## GINGER SPICE SNAPS

Put 50 g butter, $1/4$ cup soft brown sugar and 2 tablespoons golden syrup in a small heavy-based pan. Stir over low heat until the butter has melted and sugar dissolved. Remove from the heat and stir in $1/4$ cup plain flour, 1–2 teaspoons ground ginger and 1 teaspoon mixed spice. Stir until smooth and then drop teaspoonsful onto lightly greased non-stick baking trays. Only cook two snaps on each tray and cook no more than four in total at any one time. Allow plenty of room for spreading. Bake in a preheated 180°C oven for 5–7 minutes or until lightly browned and spread. Leave on the trays for about 30 seconds, then lift off with a small palette knife and cool on a wire rack. Makes about 30.

## SPICED CHERRY BRANDY PARFAIT

Put 1 cup water, $1/4$ cup sugar, 2 tablespoons soft brown sugar, 1 teaspoon mixed spice and 2–3 tablespoons brandy in a pan. Stir over low heat without boiling until all the sugar has dissolved. Bring to the boil, reduce the heat and add 520 g pitted fresh cherries. Simmer for 10 minutes, remove from the heat, cover and cool. Spoon scoops of vanilla ice cream alternately with the cherries into tall glasses. Spoon extra cherry syrup over the top. Serve with Ginger Spice Snaps or Golden Nut Cakes. Serves 6.

*From left: Warm Caramel, Nut and Banana Parfait; Golden Nut Cakes; Rich Chocolate Parfait; Mango and Macaroon Parfait; Ginger Spice Snaps; Spiced Cherry Brandy Parfait*

# Parfaits and Biscuits

## MOCHA CUSTARD PARFAIT

Put 3 teaspoons custard powder and 2 tablespoons sugar in a pan. Blend in 1 cup each of milk and cream. Stir in 1/3 cup roasted coffee beans. Stir over low heat until the mixture boils and thickens slightly. Cover the surface of the custard with plastic wrap to stop a skin forming and leave to stand for at least 10 minutes. Strain through a fine sieve into a clean pan and discard the coffee beans. Reheat the custard gently and add 50 g chopped dark chocolate and 2 tablespoons Bailey's Irish Cream, stirring until smooth. Remove from the heat and allow to cool. Put small cubes of dark chocolate mud cake in the base of each dessert glass. Drizzle over a little Bailey's Irish Cream. Top with scoops of vanilla ice cream and Mocha Custard and then decorate with chocolate-coated coffee beans. Serves 4–6.

*From left: Flaked Almond Toffee Glass; Mocha Custard Parfait; Macadamia and Berry Parfait; Tropical Coconut Parfait; Sweet Almond Macaroons; Chocolate and Marsala Parfait*

## MACADAMIA AND BERRY PARFAIT

Combine 250 g each of fresh blueberries and raspberries in a large bowl. Remove the stalks from 250 g strawberries and cut into halves, or slices if the strawberries are big. Add these to the bowl and sprinkle with 1–2 tablespoons of sugar (depending on the tartness of the berries). Pour over 1/4 cup Kirsch or your own favourite fruit liqueur and toss to cover the berries. Cover and refrigerate for at least 2 hours. Carefully beat together 1 litre softened vanilla and macadamia nut ice cream with 250 g mascarpone cheese. It's not necessary to completely mix the mascarpone through—don't worry if it looks a little lumpy. Return to the freezer until firm. Spoon scoops of ice cream alternately with berries into dessert glasses and serve immediately. Serves 6–8.

## TROPICAL COCONUT PARFAIT

Dissolve an 85 g packet of passionfruit jelly crystals as instructed on the packet. Pour into a shallow baking tin and refrigerate until set. Remove the skin from a small ripe pineapple and cut the flesh into chunks. Put in a bowl with the pulp of 3 passionfruit, 1 tablespoon soft brown sugar and 2–3 tablespoons Malibu or coconut-flavoured liqueur. Cover and chill while the jelly is setting. Cut the jelly into cubes with a spatula. Crumble some plain butter sponge, coconut or almond cake into the bottom of 4–6 dessert glasses. Layer the pineapple mixture and jelly cubes with custard (use home- or ready-made) in the glasses. Put two layers of each, finishing with custard. Top with whipped cream and toasted flaked coconut. Serve with macaroons. Serves 4–6 (depending on the size of the glasses).
Note: As an alternative, try adding chopped fresh mango or drained peach slices to the fruit mixture of pineapple and passionfruit.

## FLAKED ALMOND TOFFEE GLASS

Put 1/2 cup sugar and 2 tablespoons water in a pan and stir gently over low heat, without boiling, until dissolved. Simmer for 4–8 minutes, or until golden. Stir in 1 teaspoon ground cinnamon and pour onto a foil-lined baking tray. Hold the corner of the tray with a tea towel and tilt it to spread the toffee evenly. Quickly sprinkle over 1/4 cup of lightly toasted flaked almonds before the toffee sets. Allow to set, break into pieces and sprinkle with icing sugar.

## CHOCOLATE AND MARSALA PARFAIT

Crumble 2–3 chocolate chip fudge cookies into each dessert glass. Drizzle 2–3 teaspoons of Marsala into each glass and sprinkle with grated chocolate. Spoon or pour over some home- or ready-made custard. Top with fresh blueberries or blackberries, sliced strawberries and scoops of chocolate ice cream. Dust with combined icing sugar and dark cocoa and decorate with chocolate curls or leaves.

## SWEET ALMOND MACAROONS

Mix 100 g ground almonds with 1 cup caster sugar and 2 egg whites with electric beaters for 5 minutes. Beat in 1 tablespoon plain flour and 2 teaspoons vanilla essence until smooth. Add some grated orange or lemon rind at this point if you like. Line 2 large baking trays with non-stick baking paper. Spoon the mixture onto the trays, about 2 teaspoons per macaroon, allowing plenty of room for them to spread. Bake in a preheated 160°C oven for 20 minutes, or until crisp. Leave on the trays for 5 minutes then transfer to a wire rack to cool. Makes 25–30

# LUSCIOUS DESSERTS

## ZUCCOTTO

Preparation time: 1 hour +
  overnight chilling
Total cooking time: Nil
Serves 6–8

1 slab sponge cake (about
  30 x 25 x 2 cm)
1/3 cup Kirsch
1/4 cup Cointreau
1/3 cup rum, Cognac, Grand
  Marnier or maraschino
2 cups thickened cream
90 g dark roasted almond
  chocolate, chopped
3/4 cup finely chopped mixed
  glacé fruit
100 g dark chocolate, melted
70 g roasted hazelnuts, chopped
cocoa powder and icing sugar,
  to decorate

**1** Line a 6-cup pudding basin with damp muslin. Cut the cake into curved pieces with a sharp knife (you will need about 12 pieces). Work with one strip of cake at a time, lightly brushing it with the combined liqueurs and arranging the pieces closely in the basin. Put the thin ends in the centre so the slices cover the base and side of the basin. Brush with the remaining liqueur to soak the cake. Chill.

**2** Beat the cream into stiff peaks then divide in half. Fold the almond chocolate and glacé fruit into one half. Spread evenly over the cake in the basin, leaving a space in the centre.

**3** Fold the cooled melted chocolate and hazelnuts into the remaining cream and spoon into the centre cavity, packing it in firmly. Smooth the surface, cover and chill overnight to allow the cream to firm slightly.

**4** Turn out onto a serving plate and decorate by dusting generously with cocoa powder and icing sugar. You can make a cardboard template to help you dust separate wedges neatly—you may need help holding it in place. Serve immediately as the cream mixture will soften quickly.

### COOK'S FILE

**Storage time:** Best made one or two days in advance to give the flavours time to develop while chilling.
**Note:** Zuccotto means pumpkin, which is what the outer surface of the cake resembles. It is a rich dessert and any combination of liqueurs can be used—amaretto is also delicious.

*Cut the cake into curved pieces with a sharp knife (or use a template).*

*If you make a template to dust the cake you may need help holding it in place.*

## DOUBLE CHOCOLATE MOUSSE

Preparation time: 45 minutes + chilling
Total cooking time: 5 minutes
Serves 6

250 g white chocolate, melted
90 g dark chocolate, broken
15 g butter
2 eggs, separated
1 tablespoon brandy
1 cup cream, whipped to
    soft peaks

**1** Cut freezer wrap into six 16 cm squares. Put the white chocolate in a bowl standing in warm water to stop it hardening and, working with one sheet at a time, spread 6 circles of white chocolate onto the freezer wrap. Drape each piece over the rim of a glass, chocolate side up.
**2** When set, carefully peel away the freezer wrap. Keep the chocolate ramekins refrigerated.
**3** To make the mousse, melt the dark chocolate with the butter in a double saucepan (or a heatproof bowl over a pan of gently simmering water).

Whisk in the egg yolks and brandy and allow to cool. Fold in half the cream. Beat the egg whites until soft peaks form and fold lightly into the mousse until well combined. Fold in the remaining cream to make a swirled pattern. Spoon into the chocolate cups and chill for several hours before serving. Good with fresh dates.

### COOK'S FILE

**Hint:** When you melt chocolate in a bowl over hot water, the chocolate will overheat if the base of the bowl is touching the water.

*Spread circles of melted white chocolate onto freezer wrap.*

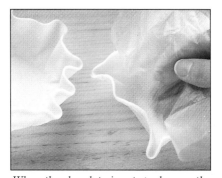

*When the chocolate is set, peel away the freezer wrap.*

*Lightly fold the beaten egg whites into the chocolate mousse.*

*Whisk the egg yolks, sugar, cornflour and lemon juice until thick and pale.*

*Heat until the mixture thickens slightly and will coat the back of a spoon.*

*Spread a layer of dried beans or rice evenly over the paper and bake blind.*

*Cover the cooked pastry edges with a ring of foil to stop them burning.*

## LEMON BRULEE TARTS

Preparation time: 40 minutes + chilling
Total cooking time: 35 minutes
Serves 4

1¹/4 cups thickened cream
2 teaspoons grated lemon rind
4 egg yolks
2 tablespoons caster sugar
2 teaspoons cornflour
2 tablespoons lemon juice
2 sheets puff pastry, thawed
¹/3 cup sugar
seasonal fruits such as berries, pawpaws, persimmons or mangoes, to serve

**1** Heat the cream in a pan with the lemon rind until almost boiling. Allow to cool slightly. Whisk the egg yolks, sugar, cornflour and lemon juice in a bowl until thick and pale.

**2** Add the cream gradually, whisking constantly. Strain into a clean pan and stir over low heat until thickened slightly—the mixture should coat the back of a wooden spoon. Pour into a heatproof bowl, cover with plastic wrap and refrigerate for several hours or overnight.

**3** Preheat the oven to 210°C. Lightly grease four 12 cm round shallow loose-bottomed tart tins. Cut 2 rounds of pastry from each sheet to line the tins. Trim the edges and prick the bases with a fork. Line these with greaseproof paper and spread a layer of dried beans or rice evenly over the paper. Bake for 15 minutes, discard the paper and beans and return to the oven for a further 5 minutes, or until lightly golden. Leave to cool.

**4** Using a tart tin as a guide, cut four foil rings a little bigger than the tin. These will protect the pastry cases to avoid burning. Spoon lemon custard into each pastry shell, smooth the top and do not overfill. Cover the edges with foil rings and sprinkle sugar generously over the surface of the custard. Cook under a preheated grill until the sugar just begins to colour. Serve immediately with fruit.

### COOK'S FILE

**Hint:** When grilling the tarts put them close to the grill so they brown quickly, but watch carefully that they do not burn. The lemon custard and pastry cases can be made up to three days ahead and the tarts assembled just before serving.

## MASCARPONE TRIFLE

Preparation time: 40 minutes + chilling
Total cooking time: 10 minutes
Serves 4–6

175 g plain sponge cake
1/2 cup Tia Maria or Kahlua
70 g dark chocolate, grated
500 g strawberries, hulled

*Custard*
4 egg yolks
2 tablespoons sugar
2 teaspoons cornflour
1/2 cup cream
1/2 cup milk
2 teaspoons vanilla essence
1 1/3 cups cream
250 g mascarpone cheese

**1** Cut the cake into chunks. Put in the base of a 7-cup capacity dish. Spoon the liqueur over the cake and sprinkle with half the grated chocolate. Slice a third of the strawberries and sprinkle over. Cover and refrigerate.

**2 To make the Custard:** Whisk together the yolks, sugar and cornflour until thick and pale. Heat the 1/2 cup cream and the milk in a pan until almost boiling, then gradually whisk into the yolk mixture. Pour into the pan and return to low heat, stirring constantly until the custard thickens and coats the back of a spoon. Remove from the heat, stir in the vanilla essence and remaining grated chocolate until smooth. Cover the surface with plastic wrap to stop a skin forming and allow to cool.

**3** Whip a third of the cream until soft peaks form and gently fold this and the mascarpone into the cooled custard. Do not beat or it may curdle.

Spoon over the cake and strawberries, cover with plastic wrap and then refrigerate until needed. When you are ready to serve, whip the remaining cream until stiff peaks form and spoon over the trifle. Cut the remaining strawberries in half and arrange on top. If you like, dust with a mixture of cocoa powder and icing sugar or spoon over some passionfruit pulp.

*Slice a third of the strawberries and layer over the cake and chocolate.*

*Gradually whisk the heated milk and cream into the yolk mixture.*

*Gently fold the cream and mascarpone into the cooled custard.*

## PEACH BAKLAVA

Preparation time: 40 minutes
Total cooking time: 20–25 minutes
Serves 8

6 sheets filo pastry
60 g butter, melted
2/3 cup slivered almonds
1 1/2 teaspoons ground
 cinnamon
1/2 cup soft brown sugar
3/4 cup orange juice, strained

4 peaches
icing sugar, to dust

**1** Preheat the oven to 180°C. Cut each sheet of pastry into 8 squares. Line eight 1-cup muffin tins with 3 layers of filo pastry—brush the pieces with melted butter to stick them together and overlap the sheets at angles.
**2** Combine the almonds, cinnamon and half the sugar. Sprinkle over the bases then cover with the 3 final squares of filo brushed with butter. Bake for 10–15 minutes.

**3** Meanwhile dissolve the remaining sugar in the orange juice, bring to the boil, reduce the heat and simmer. Halve the peaches and slice thinly, add to the syrup and stir gently to coat the fruit. Simmer for 2–3 minutes; lift from the pan with a slotted spoon. Arrange the peaches on the pastries, dust with icing sugar and serve with clotted cream or ice cream.

### COOK'S FILE

**Note:** Tinned peaches can be used if fresh are not available.

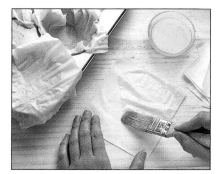

*Brush the filo squares with melted butter and use three to line each tin.*

*Sprinkle combined almonds, cinnamon and half the sugar over pastry bases.*

*Remove the peaches from the syrup with a slotted spoon.*

## CASSATA

Preparation time: 50 minutes +
   overnight freezing
Total cooking time: Nil
Serves 8

1 litre good vanilla ice cream
500 g good chocolate ice cream
1/3 cup chopped glacé fruit
1 tablespoon Grand Marnier
   or Cointreau
1/2 cup cream, whipped
1 teaspoon vanilla essence
1 egg white, beaten
1 tablespoon icing sugar
2 tablespoons chopped roasted
   pistachio nuts

**1** Put a 1.5 litre cake tin or domed mould in the freezer. Leave the vanilla ice cream at room temperature for about 10 minutes, or until softened enough to be spread easily but firmly inside the mould, to coat the base and sides. Return to the freezer for about 20 minutes. Soften the chocolate ice cream slightly and spread evenly over the vanilla ice cream. Freeze again for about 20 minutes, or until firm.

**2** Meanwhile, combine the glacé fruit and liqueur and set aside. Beat the cream and vanilla essence until firm peaks form. In a separate bowl and with clean beaters, beat the egg white into soft peaks and add the icing sugar gradually. Fold the egg white mixture into the cream, then fold in

the fruit and nuts. Fill the centre of the mould with the cream and smooth the surface. Cover with foil and freeze for at least 6 hours, or overnight.

**3** Remove Cassata from the freezer 10 minutes before serving to allow it to soften slightly. Run a spatula around the edge of the mould and invert onto a serving plate.

### COOK'S FILE

**Storage time:** Will keep frozen for up to one month.

**Hint:** An easy way to turn the Cassata out is to lay a hot damp cloth over the mould and keep reheating the cloth until the mould lifts away. Try not to melt the outside of the Cassata too much.

*Use the back of a spoon to coat the base and sides with vanilla ice cream.*

*Fill the centre of the mould with the cream and then smooth the surface.*

*Run a small spatula around the edge of the mould before inverting onto a plate.*

## FARMHOUSE RHUBARB PIE

Preparation time: 40 minutes + chilling
Total cooking time: 50 minutes
Serves 6

1½ cups plain flour, sifted
125 g chilled butter, chopped
2 tablespoons icing sugar
1 egg yolk
1 cup sugar
6 cups chopped rhubarb
2 cups peeled and sliced apple
2 teaspoons grated lemon rind
3 pieces preserved ginger, sliced
2 teaspoons sugar
sprinkle of cinnamon

**1** Process the flour, butter and icing sugar in a food processor until crumbly. Add the yolk and 1 tablespoon water and process until the dough comes together. Wrap in plastic wrap and refrigerate for 15 minutes if very soft. Preheat the oven to 190°C. Roll the pastry out to a rough 35 cm circle and put in a greased 20 cm pie plate, leaving the extra pastry to hang over the edge. Refrigerate while you prepare the filling.

**2** Heat the sugar and ½ cup water in a pan until syrupy (4–5 minutes). Add the rhubarb, apple, lemon rind and ginger, then cover and simmer for 5 minutes, until the rhubarb is cooked but still holds its shape.

**3** Drain off the liquid and cool the rhubarb. Spoon into the pastry base and sprinkle with the sugar and cinnamon. Fold the overhanging pastry roughly over the fruit and bake for 40 minutes, or until golden. Dust with icing sugar and serve. Delicious with ice cream or custard.

*Add the egg yolk and 1 tablespoon water and process until it comes together.*

*Simmer until the rhubarb is tender but still holds its shape.*

*Fold the overhanging pastry roughly over the fruit.*

## CHILLED BERRY SOUFFLE

Preparation time: 35 minutes + chilling
Total cooking time: Nil
Serves 6

1 tablespoon brandy or
  fruit liqueur
5 teaspoons gelatine
1¼ cups thickened cream
4 eggs, separated
2–3 tablespoons caster sugar
1 cup mashed raspberries

**1** Prepare six ¹/2–cup capacity soufflé dishes by tying a double strip of baking paper around the outside of each, extending 2 cm above the rim.
**2** Put the brandy in a small heatproof bowl with 2 tablespoons of hot water. Sprinkle with the gelatine and then stand in a larger bowl of warm water, stirring until dissolved. Cool slightly.
**3** Beat the cream until soft peaks form. In a separate bowl, beat the egg whites into soft peaks. Gradually beat in at least 2 tablespoons of the sugar until dissolved. Beat in the egg yolks.

If the raspberries are quite tart, add the remaining sugar to the egg white. Fold the egg mixture lightly into the cream, trying not to lose the volume. Lightly fold in the combined gelatine mixture and the raspberries. Spoon into the dishes and chill for several hours, until set. Peel away the paper and serve with cream and raspberries.

### COOK'S FILE

**Hint:** When adding a gelatine mixture to another, both must be the same temperature or lumps will form.

*Tie double thickness baking paper around the dishes to make paper collars.*

*Sprinkle the gelatine over the combined brandy and water.*

*Fold in the lightly mashed raspberries—if they are tart you will need more sugar.*

Bake for 15–20 minutes or until the cake feels spongy to the touch.

Beat in the cooled dark chocolate to make the Dark Chocolate Cream.

Cut the cakes in half and brush the cut surfaces with rum.

Spread the layers of cake with White and Dark Chocolate Cream.

## HAZELNUT TORTE

Preparation time: 50 minutes
Total cooking time: 30 minutes
Serves 8–10

6 egg whites
1¼ cups caster sugar
180 g ground hazelnuts
2 tablespoons plus 2 teaspoons
     plain flour, sifted
100 ml white rum
chopped hazelnuts

*White Chocolate Cream*
125 g white chocolate
1¾ cups thickened cream

*Dark Chocolate Cream*
40 g dark chocolate
½ cup thickened cream

**1** Grease, line and flour two 20 cm sandwich tins. Preheat the oven to 180°C. Beat the egg whites until stiff peaks form. Gradually add the sugar, beating until thick and glossy. Lightly fold in the ground hazelnuts and flour. Divide evenly between the prepared tins and smooth. Bake for 15–20 minutes, or until the cakes feel spongy to touch. Leave in the tins to cool a little before turning out onto wire racks. Split each cake in half horizontally.

**2 To make the White Chocolate Cream:** Melt the white chocolate in a double saucepan (or a heatproof bowl over a pan of gently simmering water) and allow to cool. Whip the cream until it begins to hold its shape and then beat in the chocolate. Allow to cool. Make the Dark Chocolate Cream in the same way.

**3** Put a layer of cake on a serving plate, brush the cut surface with rum and spread with a quarter of the White Chocolate Cream.

**4** Top with a second cake layer. Brush with rum and spread with all the Dark Chocolate Cream. Add another layer of cake and spread with rum and White Chocolate Cream. Top with the final cake layer and spread the remaining White Chocolate Cream over the top and side of the cake.

Decorate the Torte with the chopped hazelnuts and, perhaps, some large white chocolate leaves (see page 5 for instructions on coating leaves).

## CROQUEMBOUCHE

Preparation time: 1 hour 30 minutes
Total cooking time: 1 hour 30 minutes
Serves 10–12

100 g butter
1¹/2 cups plain flour, sifted
6 eggs, beaten
4 cups sugar

*Filling*
1¹/2 cups milk
1 vanilla bean
3 egg yolks
¹/4 cup caster sugar
2 tablespoons plain flour
¹/4 cup Grand Marnier
1¹/2 cups thickened cream

**1** Preheat the oven to 210°C. Put the butter in a large heavy-based pan with 1¹/2 cups of water and stir over medium heat until the mixture comes to the boil. Remove from the heat and quickly beat in the flour. Return to the heat and continue beating until the mixture comes together and leaves the side of the pan. Allow to cool slightly.

**2** Beat the mixture to release any more heat. Gradually add the beaten egg about 3 teaspoons at a time. Beat well between each addition until all the egg has been added and the mixture is thick and glossy—a wooden spoon should stand upright in it. (If it is too runny, the egg has been added too quickly. Beat for several minutes more, or until thickened.) Sprinkle three baking trays with water. Spoon the mixture onto the trays, leaving plenty of room for spreading. You will need about eight large puffs—vary the remainder, gradually reducing the size. One small puff is equal to about 1 heaped teaspoonful of mixture. Sprinkle the puffs lightly with a little water—this creates steam, helping the puffs to rise and the outer surface become crisp. Bake for 20 minutes, then reduce the heat to 180°C and bake for a further 50 minutes. Turn the oven off and leave the puffs inside to dry out. (You may need to prepare and cook them in two batches.)

**3 To make Filling:** Put the milk and vanilla bean in a pan. Heat gently until the milk almost boils. Remove from the heat and cool slightly. Beat the yolks, sugar and flour until thick and pale. Gradually whisk in the warm milk. Stir over medium heat until the custard boils and thickens. Remove from the heat and stir in the liqueur. Discard the vanilla bean. Cover the surface of the custard with plastic wrap to prevent a skin forming and leave to cool completely.

**4** Whip the cream into stiff peaks and fold into the custard; put into a piping bag with a nozzle less than 1 cm. Poke a small hole in the base of each puff and fill with custard.

**5** Put 2 cups of the sugar in a pan with 1 cup of water. Stir over low heat without boiling until dissolved. Simmer over low heat until the toffee is light gold (it can burn quickly).

**6** To assemble, begin with the large puffs. Dip the base of each in enough toffee to coat it and arrange in a large circle, with the sides touching. It is not necessary to have any in the centre. Build up into a cone shape, using smaller puffs nearer the top.

**7** Make the rest of the toffee and then dip two forks in it. Rub the backs of the forks together until tacky, then gently pull them apart. Spin toffee around the Croquembouche as shown on page 5.

*Quickly beat the flour into the boiling water and butter using a wooden spoon.*

*Beat in the eggs a little at a time, beating well after each addition.*

*If the mixture is ready, you should be able to stand a wooden spoon in it.*

Gradually whisk the warm milk into the egg yolks, sugar and flour mixture.

Use a small sharp knife to poke a hole in the base of each puff.

Dip the bases of the puffs in toffee to help them stick together in a cone shape.

## COINTREAU BREAD AND BUTTER PUDDINGS WITH ORANGE CREAM

Preparation time: 40 minutes +
  soaking
Total cooking time: 30 minutes
Serves 4

1/2 cup muscatels
1/3 cup Cointreau
5 eggs
1/3 cup honey
1 cup milk
1 cup cream
1 loaf crusty white bread

*Orange Cream*
1 cup whipping cream
2 teaspoons icing sugar
2 teaspoons Cointreau
grated rind of 1 orange
sprinkle of ground nutmeg

**1** Soak the muscatels in Cointreau for 2 hours, or overnight. Drain, reserving the liquid. Preheat the oven to 180°C. Beat together the eggs, honey, milk, cream and reserved Cointreau. Grease four 1-cup ramekins and divide half the muscatels among the ramekins.
**2** Slice the bread thickly. Put a slice in each ramekin, trimming to fit, sprinkle over the remaining muscatels and top with another slice of bread. Pour the egg mixture in over the top. Put the ramekins in a baking dish and pour water into the dish to come halfway up the sides of the ramekins. Bake for 25–30 minutes, or until set.
**3** Leave to stand for 5 minutes, before turning out. Serve with a dollop of Orange Cream.
**4 To make the Orange Cream:** Whip together the cream and icing sugar until peaks form. Fold in the Cointreau, rind and nutmeg.

### COOK'S FILE

**Variation:** Use sultanas instead of muscatels.

*Put a layer of muscatels, a slice of bread and then another layer of muscatels.*

*Pour water into the baking dish to make a* bain-marie.

*Run a knife around the edge of the puddings before turning them out.*

# DEEP FRIED FRUIT WITH GOLDEN NUT SAUCE

Preparation time: 55 minutes + chilling
Total cooking time: 30 minutes
Serves 6

1³/4 cups plain flour, sifted
2¹/2 teaspoons baking powder
2 tablespoons oil
2 tablespoons caster sugar
2 eggs, separated
oil, for deep frying
500 g dried fruit (figs, pitted
    dates or prunes)

*Golden Nut Sauce*
125 g butter
1 cup soft brown sugar
¹/2 cup thick pure cream
2 teaspoons lemon juice
2 tablespoons chopped roasted
    macadamias

**1** Combine the flour, baking powder, oil and sugar in a food processor. With the motor running, gradually pour in 1 cup warm water. When smooth, pour into a bowl, cover and refrigerate for 2 hours. If the batter seems a little too thick just add some more water.

**2 To make Golden Nut Sauce:** Melt the butter in a small pan over low heat. Add the sugar and stir until dissolved. Add the cream and lemon juice. Bring to the boil, stirring. Add the nuts and keep warm.

**3** Whip the egg whites until stiff and fold into the batter with the yolks. Heat the oil, dip the fruit in the batter and then deep fry in small batches, draining on paper towels. Serve immediately, drizzled with Golden Nut Sauce, with ice cream or cream.

*Leaving the motor running, slowly pour in 1 cup of water.*

*Add the chopped macadamias to the golden sauce.*

*Deep fry the fruit in small batches, draining on paper towels.*

## STICKY DATE PUDDING WITH CARAMEL SAUCE

Preparation time: 30 minutes
Total cooking time: 1 hour 10 minutes
Serves 6–8

2 cups chopped pitted dates
1 1/2 teaspoons bicarbonate
    of soda
1 teaspoon grated fresh ginger
90 g butter
1 cup caster sugar
3 eggs
1 1/2 cups self-raising flour
1/4 teaspoon ground cloves
1/2 teaspoon mixed spice
crème fraîche, for serving

*Caramel Sauce*
150 g butter
1 cup soft brown sugar
1/3 cup golden syrup
3/4 cup thickened cream

**1** Preheat the oven to 180°C. Grease and line the base of a 23 cm deep round cake tin. Put the dates in a pan with 1 3/4 cups water, bring to the boil then remove from the heat. Add the bicarbonate of soda and ginger and leave to stand for 5 minutes. Coarsely mash with a potato masher.

**2** Cream together the butter, sugar and 1 egg. Beat in the remaining eggs one at a time. Fold in the sifted flour and spices, add the date mixture and stir until well combined. Pour into the tin and bake for 55–60 minutes, or until a skewer comes out clean when inserted into the middle. Cover with foil if overbrowning during cooking. Leave to stand for 5 minutes before turning out onto a serving plate.

**3 To make Caramel Sauce:** Put all the ingredients in a pan and stir over low heat until the sugar has dissolved. Simmer, uncovered, for about 3 minutes, or until thickened slightly. Brush some sauce over the top and sides of the pudding until well-glazed. Serve immediately with the sauce and a dollop of crème fraîche.

### COOK'S FILE

**Storage time:** Best served on the day it is made. Sauce can be made up to a week ahead and refrigerated.
**Note:** Crème fraîche is a thick, rich cultured cream. Make your own by combining equal quantities of plain yoghurt and sour cream. Leave to stand overnight, without refrigerating.

*Coarsely mash the date and ginger mixture with a potato masher.*

*Once the eggs are well beaten in, gently fold in the sifted flour and the spices.*

*Stir the sauce over low heat until the sugar has dissolved.*

## RED WINE JELLY WITH FROSTED FRUITS

Preparation time: 20 minutes +
  3 hours chilling
Total cooking time: 5 minutes
Serves 4

2¹/2 cups good red wine
peel and juice of 1 orange
peel of 1 lemon
2 cinnamon sticks

¹/2 cup caster sugar
5 teaspoons gelatine
1 egg white
caster sugar, for frosting
1¹/2 cups black and red currants
  or mixed seedless grapes

**1** Combine the wine, peels, cinnamon and sugar in a small pan. Heat gently until the sugar has dissolved. Put the orange juice in a small bowl and sprinkle with the gelatine. Leave for 2 minutes. Put the bowl into a larger bowl of hot water, leave to soften slightly and then stir with a fork until the gelatine is dissolved.
**2** Stir the gelatine into the wine mixture. Pour through a muslin-lined strainer into a wetted 6¹/2-cup mould. Refrigerate until set (about 3 hours).
**3** Whisk the egg white lightly in a bowl. Put the caster sugar in another bowl. Dip the fruit first into the egg, then into the sugar, shaking off the excess. Dry on non-stick paper. Turn out the jelly and serve with the fruit.

*Stir the gelatine over a larger bowl of hot water until it has dissolved.*

*Strain the wine mixture into the mould through a sieve lined with muslin.*

*Dip the fruit into the egg white and then the sugar and dry on non-stick paper.*

## BANANA CARAMEL CREPE TOWER

Preparation time: 45 minutes + 1 hour
Total cooking time: 20 minutes
Serves 4–6

1¼ cups plain flour
pinch salt
3 eggs, beaten
1½ cups milk
1 tablespoon brandy
20 g butter, melted, plus
    extra for frying
5 bananas
1 cup chopped pecans

*Caramel Sauce*
40 g butter
½ cup soft brown sugar
½ cup condensed milk
⅓ cup golden syrup
1 cup cream, warmed

**1** Sift together the flour and salt, make a well in the centre and add the combined egg and milk. Stir from the centre, drawing in the flour a little at a time. Beat until smooth. Stir in the brandy and butter, cover and leave the batter to stand for 1 hour.

**2 To make the Caramel Sauce:** Put the butter, sugar, condensed milk and syrup in a saucepan and stir continuously over low heat until the sugar has dissolved. Bring to the boil. When the sauce has darkened slightly blend in the warmed cream, stirring for 2 minutes.

**3** Heat a 20 cm heavy-based frying pan and grease with the extra butter. Pour in just enough batter to cover the pan and pour off any excess. Heat gently and when small bubbles appear flip the crepe over using a spatula and cook the other side. The batter should make about 10–12 crepes. Keep the crepes warm by stacking them under foil until ready to serve. Slice the bananas thinly. Put a crepe on a serving plate and top with some banana and chopped pecan. Drizzle with Caramel Sauce. Put another crepe on top and repeat. Continue to layer, topping the final crepe with the remaining Caramel Sauce and pecans.

*Stir the brandy and melted butter into the batter mixture.*

*Blend the warm cream into the sauce and stir for 2 minutes.*

*Pour in just enough batter to cover the base of the hot pan.*

## IRISH COFFEE CREME CARAMEL

Preparation time: 30 minutes +
  overnight chilling
Total cooking time: 55 minutes
Serves 6–8

½ cup + ⅓ cup caster sugar
6 eggs
1 cup milk
1¼ cups cream
2 teaspoons instant coffee
¾ cup Bailey's Irish Cream

**1** Preheat the oven to 160°C. Put the ½ cup sugar with ½ cup water in a small pan and stir continuously over low heat, until dissolved. Bring to the boil, reduce the heat and simmer without stirring, for 4 minutes, or until a rich caramel colour. Pour immediately into an ungreased, deep, 20 cm round cake tin, swirling the tin so the caramel coats the base and a little up the side (hold the tin with a tea towel as it will become hot).

**2** Whisk the eggs in a large bowl with the ⅓ cup sugar until well combined. Put the milk, cream and coffee

in a pan, bring to the boil, then remove from the heat and add the Irish Cream. Gradually whisk this into the egg custard mixture. Strain and pour into the cake tin.

**3** Put the tin in a large baking dish and pour boiling water into this to come halfway up the side of the tin and make a *bain-marie*. Bake for 35–40 minutes, or until just set and a sharp knife comes out clean when inserted. Remove from the baking dish, allow to cool and refrigerate overnight. Carefully run a knife around the edge before turning out.

*Swirl the caramel to coat the base of the tin and a little up the side.*

*Carefully strain the creamy custard mixture into the tin.*

*The Crème Caramel is cooked when a knife inserted into it comes out clean.*

## CHOCOLATE SPIRAL CAKE

Preparation time: 1 hour 30 minutes
Total cooking time: 25–30 minutes
Serves 6–8

*Pastry Base*
1 cup plain flour
1/3 cup icing sugar
75 g butter, chopped
1 egg yolk
1/2 teaspoon lemon juice
2 tablespoons apricot jam

*Sponge*
6 eggs
2/3 cup caster sugar
1 1/2 cups self-raising flour
2 tablespoons cocoa powder

*Buttercream*
1/3 cup cream
150 g white chocolate melts
200 g butter
3/4 cup icing sugar
2 tablespoons coffee liqueur
1 tablespoon instant coffee powder

3/4 cup apricot jam
toasted flaked almonds, to decorate

**1** Preheat the oven to 180°C. Brush two shallow 30 x 25 cm swiss roll tins and an oven tray with melted butter or oil. Line the base and sides with non-stick baking paper. To make the pastry base, put the flour and icing sugar in a food processor. Add the butter, egg yolk, lemon juice and 1 tablespoon iced water and process until just combined. Turn onto a lightly floured surface and knead gently until smooth. Roll out on a sheet of baking paper and, using a plate as a guide, cut out an 18.5 cm circle of pastry. Chill for 15 minutes. Put the pastry on the oven tray and prick with a fork. Bake in the oven for 8–10 minutes, or until golden. Allow to cool and then spread with the 2 tablespoons of apricot jam.

**2 To make the Sponge:** Beat the eggs in a large bowl with electric beaters until thick and pale. Add the sugar gradually, beating until pale yellow and glossy and the sugar is

dissolved. Use a metal spoon to fold in the combined sifted flour and cocoa. Spread evenly into the tins and smooth the surface. Bake for 10–12 minutes, or until lightly golden and springy to the touch. Turn out onto two clean dry tea towels, covered with non-stick baking paper sprinkled with caster sugar. Remove the lining sheets of baking paper and, using the tea towels as guides, roll up the cakes from the short side with the clean baking paper. Set aside for 5 minutes, or until cooled enough to handle.

**3 To make Buttercream:** Heat the cream in a small pan until it is almost boiling. Remove from the heat and add the chocolate melts. Leave for 1–2 minutes, then stir until smooth and allow to cool. Beat the butter with electric beaters until light and creamy. Gradually add the sifted icing sugar and continue beating until well combined. Add the combined liqueur and coffee powder and then mix well. Gradually beat in the chocolate mixture until thick and creamy.

**4** To assemble, cut each roll into three 7 cm slices and remove the baking paper. Unroll one slice and spread with some of the jam, then buttercream. Trim the ends. Re-roll and place, spiral side up, in the centre of the pastry base.

**5** Continue spreading the remaining cake slices with jam and buttercream, wrapping each piece around the centre spiral until the pastry base is completely covered. Cover and refrigerate, wrapped tightly in plastic wrap, for about 1 hour. When ready to serve, transfer to a plate, spread with the remaining buttercream and decorate with toasted flaked almonds. A dusting of extra cocoa powder is a nice finishing touch.

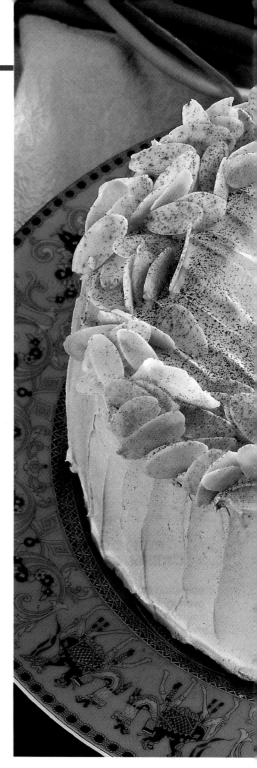

*Process the pastry mixture until it is just starting to come together.*

*Beat the sponge mixture until pale yellow and glossy and the sugar has dissolved.*

*Gradually beat in the white chocolate mixture until light and creamy.*

*Unroll one slice of the sponge and spread with jam and then buttercream.*

*Wrap each piece of sponge around the centre spiral until the base is covered.*

77

## APPLE CHARLOTTE

Preparation time: 50 minutes
Total cooking time: about 40 minutes
Serves 8

8 Granny Smith apples
1 cup caster sugar
200 ml orange juice
½ cup brandy
1 teaspoon ground cinnamon
100 g butter
50 g toasted flaked almonds
1 loaf sliced white bread
a little softened butter

**1** Peel and thinly slice the apples into a large bowl of water to prevent them discolouring. Heat the sugar with ¾ cup water in a large pan over low heat until dissolved. Bring to the boil and boil without stirring until golden brown. Remove from the heat and add the orange juice, brandy, cinnamon and butter. Drain the apples and add to the syrup. Simmer over low heat until tender, then remove the apples with a slotted spoon, set aside in a bowl and sprinkle with almonds. Boil the syrup until reduced by two-thirds.

**2** Preheat the oven to 200°C. Brush eight ½-cup ramekins with melted butter; cut 16 rounds of bread, spread with softened butter and put a round in each ramekin, buttered side down. Cut the remaining bread into wide strips, butter and use to line the sides of the ramekins, overlapping a little, buttered side against the ramekin.

**3** Reserve some slices of apple for garnishing and spoon the rest into the ramekins, pressing down firmly. Put the remaining buttered rounds of bread on top of the apple, buttered side up. Press down firmly and bake for 15 minutes, or until golden. Turn out onto individual plates to serve and top with the remaining apple. Drizzle with syrup and serve immediately.

COOK'S FILE

**Note:** Try other fruit such as pears, apricots, peaches or berries. You can use well-drained tinned fruit.

*Remove the apples with a slotted spoon and set aside in a bowl.*

*Cut the bread into circles and strips to line the bases and sides of the ramekins.*

*Bake the Apple Charlottes for 15 minutes until they are golden.*

## BLACK FOREST ICE CREAM

Preparation time: 45 minutes
Total cooking time: 10 minutes
Serves 10

425 g can pitted black cherries
200 g flaked almonds, toasted
2 litres good vanilla ice cream
200 g dark chocolate
35 g white vegetable shortening

**1** Cover 2 baking trays with foil and freeze until needed. Drain the cherries and pat dry with paper towels. Toast the almonds on a separate oven tray for 5 minutes at 180°C, until golden. Leave to cool. Push a cherry into the ice cream. Use an ice cream scoop dipped in cold water to take a scoop from around the cherry. Mould into a small ball, roll in toasted almonds and put on one of the trays in the freezer.
**2** Continue rolling and freezing until all the cherries are coated. Melt the chocolate and shortening together in a double saucepan (or a heatproof bowl standing over a pan of gently simmering water) and leave to cool a little.
**3** Quickly dip the ice cream balls in melted chocolate with a spoon and put on the tray. Work quickly and serve as soon as the chocolate has set or freeze until ready to serve.

### COOK'S FILE

**Note:** Vegetable shortening is also known as Copha.

*Use a small ice cream scoop to make a ball around each cherry.*

*Roll each moulded ice cream ball in the toasted almond flakes.*

*Quickly dip the ice cream balls in the melted chocolate.*

## PECAN PRALINE CUSTARD CUPS

Preparation time: 15 minutes + chilling
Total cooking time: 30 minutes
Serves 6–12

1¹/4 cups milk
300 ml cream
1 teaspoon vanilla essence
2 eggs, plus 2 extra egg yolks
¹/4 cup caster sugar
1¹/2 tablespoons cornflour

*Pecan Praline*
¹/2 cup toasted pecans
¹/2 cup caster sugar

**1** Put the milk, cream and vanilla in a pan. Bring to boiling point then remove from the heat. Whisk together the eggs, yolks, sugar and cornflour. Gradually whisk in the scalded milk and return to the pan. Stir over the heat, until custard boils and thickens. Simmer for 3 minutes. Pour into six 1-cup ramekins. Cover with plastic wrap to prevent a skin forming and chill for several hours, or overnight.

**2 To make the Pecan Praline:** Put the pecans on a baking tray. Bake at 180°C for 5 minutes, or until golden, and set aside to cool. Put the sugar and 2 tablespoons water in a small pan. Stir over the heat until the sugar dissolves; brush down the sides of the pan occasionally with a wet pastry brush. Simmer, without stirring, until pale golden. Pour over the toasted pecans and allow to set. Process or crush with a rolling pin and store in an airtight container until required.

**3** Before serving, sprinkle Pecan Praline generously over the custards. Place under a hot grill until golden (watch carefully as this happens quickly and it may burn). Allow to cool or refrigerate before serving with fresh fruit.

### COOK'S FILE

**Variation:** Add 90 g melted milk chocolate to the custard before cooling to make chocolate cups.

*Pour the custard cream into the small ramekins, then cover and refrigerate.*

*For the Pecan Praline, pour the toffee over the nuts on the tray.*

*Generously sprinkle the custards with chopped Pecan Praline.*

## PECAN AND MAPLE SYRUP PUDDING

Preparation time: 20 minutes
Total cooking time: 2 hours
Serves 8–10

200 g butter
1 cup caster sugar
4 eggs, lightly beaten
1 teaspoon vanilla essence
3 cups self-raising flour, sifted

200 g chopped pecans
1/2 teaspoon ground cinnamon
grated rind of lemon
3/4 cup milk
1 cup maple syrup

**1** Preheat the oven to 180°C. Beat the butter and sugar with electric beaters until creamy. Gradually beat in the eggs, then the vanilla essence. Combine the flour, pecans, cinnamon and rind and fold in, alternating with spoonfuls of milk, until smooth.

**2** Reserve 1/4 cup maple syrup and pour the rest into a 9-cup ovenproof bowl. Fill with pudding mixture and pour the remaining syrup on top.

**3** Cover with foil and put in a large baking dish. Pour enough water into the dish to come halfway up the side of the bowl and bake for 2 hours. Test with a skewer to see if the pudding is cooked in the centre—the skewer should come out clean. Turn out onto a large serving plate and serve with ice cream or cream, if desired.

*Fold through the flour, pecans, cinnamon and rind, alternating with the milk.*

*Pour the remaining maple syrup over the top of the pudding.*

*Test with a skewer to see if the pudding is cooked in the centre.*

## OLD-FASHIONED TRIFLE

Preparation time: 40 minutes + chilling
Total cooking time: 5–10 minutes
Serves 4–6

250 g packet jam rollettes
85 g packet port wine, cherry
    or strawberry jelly
1/2 cup Marsala or sweet sherry
1 large mango, peeled and
    thinly sliced
200 g fresh cherries, pitted
425 g can pear slices, drained
1 cup cream, whipped
2 tablespoons strawberry jam,
    sieved

*Custard*
1/4 cup custard powder
1/4 cup sugar
1 1/4 cups milk
3/4 cup cream
2 teaspoons vanilla essence
1/3 cup thick pure cream

**1** Cut the rollettes into thirds; layer closely over the base and a little way up the side of a 2-litre glass bowl, so the swirls can be seen. Pile the rest in the middle. Combine the jelly crystals, 1 1/2 cups boiling water and Marsala in a jug and stir until dissolved. Spoon over the rollettes—the liquid should run down the side of the bowl to soak them. Cover and refrigerate.

**2 To make the Custard:** Put the custard powder and sugar in a pan. Gradually blend in the milk and cream and stir over medium heat until the mixture boils and thickens. Stir in the vanilla essence. Cover the surface with plastic wrap to prevent a skin forming. Allow to cool before folding in the thick cream.

**3** Put a third of the fruit over the jam rollettes and spoon custard over the top. Put the remaining fruit over the custard. Cover with plastic wrap and refrigerate until needed. Just before serving, spread whipped cream over the top. Put the jam in a paper icing bag, sealing the end. Snip off the tip and pipe fine lines over the trifle. To feather, drag with a fine skewer, wiping the skewer clean each time.

### COOK'S FILE

**Note:** The flavour of a trifle is often better the day after it has been made, when the flavours have developed.

*Carefully spoon the jelly and Marsala over the rollettes to completely soak them.*

*Cover the surface of the custard with plastic wrap to stop a skin forming.*

*Create a feathered effect by dragging a fine skewer across the piped lines of jam.*

*Make a well in the centre of the flour and salt and pour in the eggs and milk.*

*Flip the crepe using a spatula and cook the other side.*

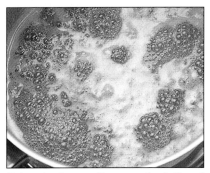

*Bring the Lemon Sauce to the boil and simmer until it becomes syrupy.*

*Deep fry the crepe ribbons until golden and drain on paper towels.*

## CREPE RIBBONS WITH ZESTY LEMON SAUCE

Preparation time: 50 minutes + 1 hour
Total cooking time: 30–40 minutes
Serves 4–6

1¼ cups plain flour, sifted
pinch of salt
3 eggs, beaten
2 cups milk
1 tablespoon brandy
20 g butter, melted
oil, for frying
icing sugar, to dust

*Zesty Lemon Sauce*
½ cup lemon juice
1 tablespoon grated lemon rind
80 g butter
½ cup caster sugar

**1** Combine the flour and salt in a bowl. Make a well in the centre and add the combined egg and milk. Stir in the flour gradually until smooth. Stir in the brandy and melted butter. Cover and leave to stand for 1 hour.
**2** Heat a small lightly greased, heavy-based frying pan. Pour in just enough batter to cover the pan. Cook gently until the underside is golden, then flip over with a spatula and cook the other side. Continue until all the batter is used, greasing the pan before making each crepe.
**3 To make Zesty Lemon Sauce:** Combine the lemon juice, rind, butter and sugar in a small pan. Bring to the boil, reduce the heat and simmer until the liquid becomes syrupy. Keep warm until ready to serve.
**4** Cut the cold crepes into ribbons about 2 cm wide. Heat the oil in a large pan and cook the ribbons in batches until crisp. Drain on paper towels. Pile up the ribbons onto individual serving plates, pour over the Zesty Lemon Sauce and dust with icing sugar. Delicious served with fruit and cream.

### COOK'S FILE

**Note:** Crepes and sauce can both be made in advance. Fry the ribbons just before serving.

## STRAWBERRY MILLE FEUILLE

Preparation time: 40 minutes
Total cooking time: 15 minutes
Serves 6

3 sheets ready-rolled puff pastry
500 g fresh strawberries
1¼ cups cream
⅓ cup icing sugar
¼ teaspoon vanilla essence
½ cup raspberry jam
    or conserve

**1** Preheat the oven to 220°C. Splash 3 baking trays with water, put a sheet of pastry on each and prick several times. Bake for 10 minutes, or until golden and crisp then turn over and bake for 2–3 minutes. Trim the edges and cut each sheet into 6 portions. Crush the pastry trimmings with a rolling pin and set aside.

**2** Cut 250 g even-sized strawberries in half and set aside. Combine the cream, icing sugar and vanilla essence and whip until firm. Slice the rest of the strawberries and fold in. Spread 6 pastry slices with half the cream.

Cover with more pastry and spread the rest of the cream over this and the sides. Top with the final pastry slices.

**3** Press the reserved crushed pastry onto the sides. Put the jam or conserve in a small pan with 2 tablespoons water and heat gently until liquid, then brush over the top of the pastry. Arrange the strawberry halves on top and brush again with conserve.

### COOK'S FILE

**Variation:** Any berries or fruit can be used and, for a special touch, mix brandy with the jam instead of water.

*Trim the edges of the pastry and cut each sheet into 6 portions.*

*Spread the rest of the cream on the top layer and over the sides.*

*Press the crushed pastry trimmings onto the sides of the Mille Feuille.*

## POACHED PEARS WITH GINGER ZABAGLIONE

Preparation time: 30 minutes
Total cooking time: 1 hour
Makes 6

2 cups good red wine
4 pieces crystallised ginger
1/2 cup sugar
6 pears, peeled

*Ginger Zabaglione*
8 egg yolks
1/3 cup caster sugar
1 teaspoon ground ginger
1 1/4 cups Marsala

**1** Put the wine, 4 cups water, ginger and sugar in a large pan and stir over medium heat until the sugar has dissolved. Add the pears, cover and simmer for 45 minutes, or until tender.

**2 To make the Zabaglione:** Put the egg yolks, sugar and ginger in a heatproof bowl and beat with electric beaters until pale yellow. Put the bowl over a gently simmering pan of water and beat continuously, adding the Marsala gradually. Beat for 5 minutes until thick and frothy. To test, dip a metal spoon into the Zabaglione: hold up the spoon and if the mixture slides down the back it is not yet thickened enough. If you can draw a line through it on the spoon, it is ready.

**3** Remove the pears from the pan with a slotted spoon. Arrange on plates and pour Ginger Zabaglione over each. Serve immediately.

### COOK'S FILE

**Hint:** Use as good a quality wine for cooking as you would for drinking.

*Add the pears to the warm mixture of wine, ginger and sugar and simmer.*

*Test to see if the pears are tender by piercing with a sharp knife.*

*The Zabaglione has thickened if you can draw a line through it on the spoon.*

## PRUNE AND ALMOND CUSTARD TART

Preparation time: about 2 hours
Total cooking time: 50 minutes
Serves 6–8

375 g pitted prunes
2/3 cup muscat or sweet sherry
1/3 cup redcurrant jelly

*Almond Shortcrust Pastry*
1 1/2 cups plain flour
1/3 cup ground almonds
1/4 cup caster sugar
125 g chilled butter, chopped
1 egg yolk
50 g marzipan, grated

*Custard Cream*
1/4 cup custard powder
1 2/3 cups milk
1/2 cup sour cream
1 tablespoon caster sugar
2 teaspoons vanilla essence

**1** Put the prunes in a pan with the muscat or sherry, leave to soak for 1 hour, then simmer over very low heat for 10 minutes, or until the prunes are tender but not mushy. Remove the prunes from the liquid with a slotted spoon and leave to cool. Add the redcurrant jelly to the pan and then stir over low heat until dissolved. Cover and set aside.

**2 To make Almond Shortcrust Pastry:** Put the flour, almonds and sugar in a food processor and process for 15 seconds. Add the butter and process for 15 seconds until crumbly. Add the egg yolk and 2–3 tablespoons iced water, until the dough just comes together. Turn out onto a lightly floured surface and knead briefly until smooth. Refrigerate for 15 minutes. Preheat the oven to 180°C and heat a baking tray.

**3** Roll out the chilled pastry between 2 sheets of non-stick baking paper until large enough to line the base and side of a lightly greased 23 cm loose-bottomed flan tin. Ease the pastry into the tin and trim the edges. (If it is still too soft it may need to be refrigerated for another 10 minutes.)

**4** Cover the pastry with a sheet of non-stick baking paper and then fill with baking beans or rice. Refrigerate for 15 minutes and then blind bake on the heated baking tray for 15 minutes. Remove the beans and paper, reduce the heat to 160°C and bake for another 5 minutes. Sprinkle marzipan over the pastry base and bake for a further 5–10 minutes, or until golden. Leave in the tin to cool.

**5 To make Custard Cream:** In a small bowl, blend the custard powder with a little milk until smooth. Transfer to a pan and add the remaining milk, sour cream and sugar. Stir over medium heat for 5–7 minutes, or until thickened. Stir in the vanilla essence, remove from the heat and cover the surface with plastic wrap to prevent a skin forming.

**6** Spread the Custard Cream, while it is still warm, evenly over the pastry case. Cut the prunes in half lengthways and arrange over the custard. Warm the redcurrant and muscat mixture and carefully spoon over the tart to cover it completely. Refrigerate for at least 2 hours to allow the custard to firm before serving.

### COOK'S FILE

**Storage time:** Prune and Almond Tart is best assembled on the same day as serving.

*Cook the prunes over low heat until they are tender but not mushy.*

*Process until the pastry mixture just comes together.*

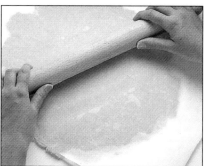

*Roll out the pastry between two sheets of non-stick baking paper.*

*Lift out the baking paper and beans or rice from the pastry base.*

*Blend the custard powder with a little milk until smooth.*

*Spread the Custard Cream evenly into the pastry base.*

## CHOCOLATE CHESTNUT LOG

Preparation time: 50 minutes
+ overnight freezing
Total cooking time: 15 minutes
Serves 10–12

150 g unsalted butter
1/3 cup caster sugar
1 cup chestnut purée
175 g dark chocolate, chopped
1/4 cup espresso coffee
1/4 cup brandy
125 g unblanched almonds
1/2 cup granulated sugar

**1** Cream together the butter and sugar; when light and creamy mix in the purée. Use a double saucepan (or a heatproof bowl over a pan of gently simmering water) to melt together the chocolate, coffee and brandy. Cool, add to the chestnut mixture and mix well. Spoon into a loaf tin lined with plastic wrap. Freeze overnight.

**2** Cover a baking tray with non-stick baking paper. Put the almonds and sugar in a heavy-based frying pan over low heat—tilt the pan but don't stir. The sugar will form lumps then melt to a caramel colour (praline burns quickly so you may need to lift it from the heat occasionally). Pour onto the tray and leave to set. Process, chop or grind with a rolling pin.

**3** Cut the chocolate mixture in half lengthways. Wrap each half tightly in plastic wrap and roll to make logs. Freeze for another 30 minutes. Unwrap and roll in the praline to evenly coat. Serve sliced.

### COOK'S FILE

**Note:** Chestnut purée is sold in cans.

*Add the cooled melted chocolate, coffee and brandy to the chestnut mixture.*

*When making the praline, tilt the pan instead of stirring.*

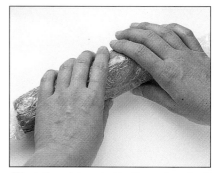

*Wrap the mixture in plastic wrap and roll each half on a flat surface to make logs.*

## HOT LIME SHORTCAKE PUDDING

Preparation time: 1 hour + chilling
Total cooking time: 1 hour 20 minutes
Serves 6

3 cups plain flour, sifted
1 1/2 teaspoons baking powder
pinch of salt
200 g chilled butter, chopped
1/2 cup desiccated coconut
250–300 ml cream
1/2 cup lime marmalade

*Hot Lime Syrup*
3/4 cup caster sugar
juice and finely grated rind
    of 3 limes
60 g butter

**1** Combine the flour, baking powder and salt. Rub in the butter until crumbly. Stir in the coconut. Use a knife to mix in almost all the cream: add the rest, if needed, to form a soft dough. Roll out between 2 sheets of baking paper to make a 25 x 40 cm rectangle. Spread with marmalade and roll up lengthways like a swiss roll and then refrigerate for 20 minutes.

**2** Preheat the oven to 180°C. Grease a 6-cup ovenproof bowl. Cut the roll into 2 cm slices and arrange to cover the base and sides of the bowl. Fill the centre with the remaining slices.

**3 For Hot Lime Syrup:** Put all the ingredients in a small pan with 3/4 cup water; stir over low heat until the sugar dissolves. Bring to the boil and pour over the cake. Put on a tray to catch drips; bake for 1 hour 15 minutes, or until a skewer comes out clean when inserted into the centre. Leave for 15 minutes before turning out.

*Use a knife to cut in almost all of the cream, adding the rest if necessary.*

*Arrange the shortcake rolls around the base and side, then fill the centre.*

*Pour the Hot Lime Syrup over the slices of shortcake.*

89

## VANILLA BEAN CREAM POTS WITH POACHED TAMARILLOS

Preparation time: 1 hour + chilling
Total cooking time: 1 hour
Serves 6

*Vanilla Bean Cream*
700 ml cream
1 vanilla bean
2 eggs
2 egg yolks
2 tablespoons caster sugar
1 teaspoon vanilla essence

*Poached Tamarillos*
6 tamarillos with stalks
1¹/2 cups caster sugar
5 cm piece orange rind
2–3 tablespoons cherry
    liqueur or Kirsch

**1** Put six ¹/2-cup ramekins in a large baking dish. Put the cream and bean in a pan, bring slowly to the boil then reduce the heat and simmer for 5 minutes. Remove from the heat, split the bean, scrape out the seeds and return the bean and seeds to the cream. Cover and leave to infuse for 30 minutes. Strain and set the cream aside.
**2** Preheat the oven to 160°C. Whisk together the eggs and yolks, sugar and vanilla essence for 1 minute. Whisk in the cream, pour into the ramekins and cover securely with foil. Pour hot water into the dish to come halfway up the ramekins. Bake for 30 minutes, or until just set—do not overcook. Leave covered and refrigerate for at least 4 hours, or overnight.
**3** To skin the tamarillos, plunge them into boiling water for 10 seconds, then put in iced water and peel away the skins, leaving the stalks attached. Put the sugar in a pan with 3 cups water and the orange rind; stir to dissolve the sugar. Bring to the boil and boil for 3 minutes. Reduce the heat to simmer and add the tamarillos. Poach for 6–8 minutes, depending on ripeness. Turn off the heat, add the liqueur and leave the fruit in the syrup to cool. When ready to serve, pour the syrup into a pan. Bring to the boil and boil for 5–10 minutes, until reduced and thickened. Pour into a jug, cover and cool (it will thicken a little more on standing). Cut each tamarillo in half, leaving the end near the stalk intact. Spoon sauce onto each plate with the tamarillo and Vanilla Bean Cream.

### COOK'S FILE

**Note:** You can use 1 teaspoon of vanilla essence in place of the bean.

*Split open the bean and run a knife down the centre to scrape out the seeds.*

*Whisk the vanilla-flavoured cream into the egg and sugar mixture.*

*Peel the skin away from the tamarillos, leaving the stalks intact.*

## PINEAPPLE SAVARIN

Preparation time: 40 minutes +
    1 hour 30 minutes rising
Total cooking time: 40 minutes
Serves 6–8

**7 g sachet dried yeast**
**2/3 cup unsweetened pineapple**
    **juice, warmed**
**2 teaspoons caster sugar**
**2 cups plain flour**
**1/4 teaspoon salt**
**3 eggs, lightly beaten**
**90 g butter, softened**

*Rum Syrup*
**1/2 cup caster sugar**

**3/4 cup unsweetened**
    **pineapple juice**
**5 cm piece lemon rind**
**1/3 cup dark rum**

**1** Grease a 25 cm deep savarin ring. Dissolve the yeast in the pineapple juice; stir in the sugar. Set aside for 5 minutes until frothy. Sift the flour and salt into a large bowl. Add the yeast and eggs and beat with a cupped hand for 5 minutes. Cover and set aside in a warm place for 45 minutes until bubbly and well-risen.
**2** Add the butter and beat by hand for 5 minutes. Ladle into the ring and cover loosely with plastic wrap. Set aside in a warm place for 45 minutes, or until well risen. Preheat the oven to 190°C. Bake on an oven tray for 25 minutes, or until firm and golden (it may overflow a little in the centre). Trim with a knife, when cooked.
**3 To make the Rum Syrup:** Put the sugar, juice and lemon rind in a small pan. Stir without boiling until the sugar has dissolved. Bring to the boil and boil without stirring for 10 minutes, or until slightly thickened. Add the rum and remove the rind. Turn out of the tin and leave to stand on a rack over a tray. Prick all over with a skewer. While the Savarin is still hot, drizzle with Rum Syrup, pouring the excess back from where it is caught in the tray, until all the syrup is absorbed. Delicious with clotted cream and fresh pineapple.

*Use your cupped hand to beat the mixture vigorously.*

*Poke holes in the Savarin with a skewer to allow the syrup to soak in.*

*Put the Savarin over a tray to catch any excess syrup as you pour.*

91

## RASPBERRY LATTICE TARTLETS

Preparation time: 50 minutes
Total cooking time: 25 minutes
Makes 8

125 g cream cheese
125 g butter
1¹/2 cups plain flour
1 egg, beaten
1 tablespoon caster sugar

*Raspberry Filling*
250 g fresh raspberries
70 g soft unsalted butter
¹/3 cup caster sugar
1 egg
70 g ground almonds

**1** Beat the cream cheese and butter until soft. Stir in the sifted flour with a knife and mix to a dough. Press together to form a ball. Lightly grease 8 small stainless-steel dishes or eight ¹/2 cup muffin tins. Roll out the pastry to 3 mm thick between 2 sheets of baking paper; cut into 8 rounds using a 10.5 cm plain cutter and ease into the dishes or tins.

**2 To make Raspberry Filling:** Divide the raspberries among the pastry cases. Cream together the butter and sugar and then beat in the egg. Fold in the almonds and spoon on top of the raspberries.

**3** Preheat the oven to 180°C. Roll out the pastry scraps and cut into 5 mm wide strips. Weave into a lattice on a board, lightly press down with the palm of your hand and cut into rounds with the 10 cm cutter. Brush the pastry rims of the tartlets with beaten egg, put the lattice rounds on top and gently press down the edges to seal. Re-roll the scraps to make more lattice until all the tartlets are topped. Glaze with beaten egg, sprinkle with a little caster sugar and bake for 20–25 minutes, or until golden.

*Stir in the sifted flour and mix to a dough with a knife.*

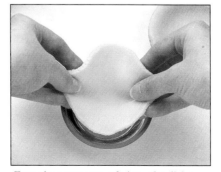

*Ease the pastry rounds into the dishes or muffin tins.*

*Brush the pastry edges with beaten egg and place the lattice on top.*

# LEMON SYRUP PEARS WITH PANCAKES

Preparation time: 40 minutes
Total cooking time: 1 hour 10 minutes
Serves 6

1 cup plain flour
$^2/_3$ cup self-raising flour
2 tablespoons caster sugar
3 eggs, lightly beaten
1$^1/_2$ cups milk
60 g butter, melted

*Lemon Syrup Pears*
5 firm pears (try buerre bosc)
1 lemon
$^3/_4$ cup caster sugar
2 tablespoons honey
$^1/_2$ cup lemon juice
1 cup sour cream

**1** Sift the flours into a bowl, add the sugar, make a well and whisk in the eggs, milk and butter. Beat until smooth then set aside for 30 minutes.

**2 To make Lemon Syrup Pears:** Peel, halve and core the pears, then cut into wedges. Peel the lemon and cut the rind into thin strips. Combine the sugar, honey and 1$^1/_2$ cups water in a pan, stirring over low heat until the sugar dissolves. Add the lemon juice, bring to the boil, reduce the heat and simmer for 8 minutes. Skim any froth, add the pears and simmer for a further 5 minutes, or until just tender. Remove from the heat, stir in the lemon rind and leave to cool slightly.

**3** Pour $^1/_4$ cup pancake batter into a lightly greased 20 cm non-stick frying pan and cook over medium heat for 2 minutes each side. Continue with the rest of the batter, greasing the pan

when necessary. Strain $^1/_2$ cup of the lemon syrup and mix with the sour cream to make a sauce for the pancakes. Strain the pears to serve and decorate with strips of lemon rind.

COOK'S FILE

**Hint:** Poached pears can be left in the syrup, covered in the refrigerator, for up to two days to allow the flavours to develop. Reheat to serve.

*Make a well in the centre and whisk in the combined egg, milk and butter.*

*Slice the pears into wedges and cut the lemon rind into thin strips.*

*Stack the cooked pancakes under a clean tea towel to keep them warm.*

## BOMBE ALASKA

Preparation time: 30 minutes +
  2 hours freezing
Total cooking time: 8 minutes
Serves 6–8

2 litres good vanilla ice cream
250 g mixed glacé fruit,
  finely chopped
1/4 cup Grand Marnier or
  Cointreau
2 teaspoons grated orange rind
60 g toasted almonds,
  finely chopped
60 g dark chocolate,
  finely chopped

1 sponge or butter cake
3 egg whites
3/4 cup caster sugar

**1** Line an 8-cup pudding basin with damp muslin. Soften 1 litre of ice cream enough to fold in the glacé fruit, 2 tablespoons liqueur and 1 teaspoon orange rind. Spoon into the basin, smooth and return to freezer. Soften the remaining ice cream and fold in the almonds, chocolate, remaining liqueur and orange rind. Spoon over the first layer and smooth.
**2** Work quickly to evenly cover the ice cream with a 3 cm thick layer of cake. Cover with foil and freeze for at least 2 hours. Preheat the oven to

220°C. Beat the egg whites in a dry bowl until soft peaks form. Gradually add the sugar, beating well after each addition. Beat for 4–5 minutes, until thick and glossy.
**3** Unmould the ice cream onto an ovenproof dish and remove the muslin. Quickly spread the meringue over the top to cover the ice cream completely. Bake in the oven for 5–8 minutes, or until lightly browned. Cut into wedges and serve at once.

### COOK'S FILE

**Hint:** Partly bury half a small egg shell in the top of the meringue before baking. After baking fill with warmed brandy and set alight to serve.

*Spoon the second layer of ice cream over the first and smooth the surface.*

*Completely cover the ice cream with a 3 cm thick layer of cake.*

*Quickly spread the meringue roughly over the top, to cover the ice cream completely.*

*Process the flours, sugar, ginger and butter until fine and crumbly.*

*The lemon juice and water will prevent the sliced apples discolouring.*

*Stir the sugar into the butter until it is all moistened, then simmer for 2 minutes.*

*Turn back the edges of the pastry and press with a fork.*

## APPLE GINGER TATIN

Preparation time: 40 minutes
Total cooking time: 1 hour 10 minutes
Serves 6–8

1½ cups plain flour
½ cup self-raising flour
2 tablespoons caster sugar
2–3 teaspoons ground ginger
90 g cold butter, chopped
1 egg yolk
2 teaspoons lemon juice
2 teaspoons lemon rind
3 tablespoons iced water

*Filling*
3 green apples
juice of half a lemon
90 g butter
2/3 cup caster sugar
1/4 cup soft brown sugar

**1** Put the flours, sugar, ginger and butter in a food processor and process until fine and crumbly. While process-ing, add the egg yolk, lemon juice, rind and enough iced water for the dough to just come together. Turn out onto a lightly floured surface and knead briefly to form a smooth dough.

**2** Peel and core the apples, cut into quarters, then cut each quarter in half. Leave in a bowl of water and lemon juice. Melt the butter in a 23 cm heavy-based frying pan with an oven-proof handle—a cast-iron pan is per-fect. Add the caster sugar, stirring to moisten, and simmer gently for 2 min-utes. Add the apple slices and sprin-kle with brown sugar. Cook over low heat for 25–30 minutes, until the but-ter and sugar begin to caramelize. Take care the apple does not burn. Remove from the heat.

**3** Preheat the oven to 210°C. Roll the pastry into a circle 2 cm larger than the rim of the pan (draw round the pan on baking paper as a guide). Press firmly onto the apple, turning the edges back with a fork. Be quick or the dough may soften too much.

**4** Bake for 15 minutes, then reduce the heat to 190°C for 15–20 minutes, or until risen and golden. Leave to stand for 15 minutes before inverting onto a plate. Serve warm with cream.

## TREACLE GINGER PUDDING WITH SWEET WINE SAUCE

Preparation time: 30 minutes
Total cooking time: about 2 hours
Serves 6–8

125 g butter
3/4 cup caster sugar
3 eggs
1/4 cup treacle
1/2 cup plain flour
2/3 cup self-raising flour
1 tablespoon ground ginger
1/3 cup sour cream
1/4 cup finely chopped
    glacé ginger

*Sweet Wine Sauce*
30 g butter
1 tablespoon plain flour
1/4 cup ginger wine
2 tablespoons soft brown sugar
1 1/2 cups cream

**1** Brush an 8-cup capacity pudding steamer or basin with melted butter or oil and line the base with non-stick baking paper. Grease a large sheet of foil and lay a large sheet of non-stick baking paper over the foil; make a pleat along the centre. This will reduce the pressure when the pudding is being steamed and allow the covering to expand a little.

**2** Beat the butter and sugar with electric beaters until light and creamy. Add the eggs, one at a time, beating well after each addition, and then beat in the treacle.

**3** Mix together the sifted flours and ground ginger and fold into the mixture with a metal spoon, alternating with spoonfuls of the sour cream. The mixture may appear to be slightly curdled at this stage. Stir in the glacé ginger. Spoon into the prepared steamer or basin.

**4** Cover with the paper and foil, paper side down, and secure with string. Cover the top with a tea towel, secure with string and knot the tea towel on top. (If your steamer has a lid, simply lay a sheet of non-stick baking paper over the basin and secure the lid over the top with clips.) Put the basin on an upturned saucer or wire rack in a large pan.

**5** Add enough boiling water to the pan to come two-thirds of the way up the side of the basin and cover with a tight-fitting lid. Boil steadily for 1 hour 30 minutes to 2 hours, or until a skewer comes out clean when inserted in the centre (poke the skewer through the foil cover so the steam can't escape if the pudding isn't cooked). Replenish the pan with extra boiling water when necessary. Do not allow the pudding to boil dry. Remove from the pan and leave in the basin for 5–10 minutes before turning out.

**6 To make Sweet Wine Sauce:** While the pudding is cooking, melt the butter in a pan, add the flour and stir for 1 minute, or until bubbling and golden. Remove from the heat and gradually stir in the combined ginger wine, sugar and cream. Return to low heat and stir for 5 minutes, or until the mixture boils and thickens. Serve warm over wedges of hot pudding. Also delicious with vanilla ice cream.

### COOK'S FILE

**Hint:** The cooking time may vary depending on the basin—ceramic may take longer than stainless steel. Any leftover pudding or sauce can be easily reheated in the microwave.

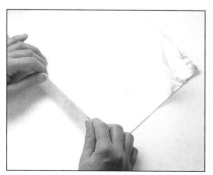

*Make a pleat along the centre of the foil and baking paper so it can expand.*

*Once you have added the eggs, beat in the treacle.*

*Fold in the flour, ginger and sour cream and don't worry if it appears curdled.*

Put the sheet of baking paper and foil over the top and secure with string.

Do not let the pan boil dry—add extra boiling water whenever necessary.

Remove the pan from the heat and stir in the ginger wine, sugar and cream.

## TRIPLE CHOCOLATE TERRINE

Preparation time: 1 hour + freezing
Total cooking time: 10minutes
Serves 8–10

150 g milk chocolate, chopped
6 eggs
³/4 cup icing sugar
60 g butter
2 cups thickened cream
150 g white chocolate, chopped
150 g dark chocolate, chopped
2 teaspoons instant coffee
3–4 teaspoons dark rum

**1** Line a 10 x 24 cm loaf tin with baking paper, extending above the tin. Melt the milk chocolate in a small bowl over a pan of simmering water, until smooth. Separate 2 of the eggs and beat the whites until soft peaks form. Gradually beat in ¹/4 cup of the icing sugar, until thick and glossy. Beat in the 2 egg yolks and the cooled melted chocolate. Melt 20 g of the butter and beat in. Whip ²/3 cup of the cream into soft peaks. Fold into the egg white mixture and then spoon into the tin, with the tin tilted on one side lengthways. Put in the freezer on this angle and leave for 1–2 hours, until just firm.

**2** Repeat the same method with the white chocolate. Spoon this mixture into the other side of the tin so that the terrine becomes level. Put the tin flat in the freezer to set.

**3** Repeat the same method with the remaining ingredients, folding in the dissolved coffee and rum with the dark chocolate. Spoon into the tin and smooth the surface. Freeze for several hours, then cut into slices to serve.

### COOK'S FILE

**Storage time :** Can be frozen for up to three months.
**Variation:** Add liqueurs of your choice to flavour each layer.

*Beat in the melted cooled chocolate and the egg yolk.*

*Spoon the white chocolate mixture into the other side of the tin.*

*Carefully stir the dissolved coffee and rum into the melted dark chocolate.*

# FRENCH TEA BUN PUDDING

Preparation time: 30 minutes
Total cooking time: 1 hour 30 minutes
Serves 4–6

1 cup whole dark or sour
   cherries in 1/2 cup juice
1/3 cup cherry jam or conserve
2 large custard or plain tea
   buns, a day or two old
3 eggs
2 tablespoons caster sugar
3/4 cup milk
1 cup cream
1 teaspoon vanilla essence
icing sugar, to dust

**1** Preheat the oven to 180°C. Brush a deep 20 cm square cake tin with oil or melted butter and line the base and 2 sides with non-stick baking paper. Drain and pit the cherries; put the juice in a pan with the jam. Stir over low heat to dissolve. Bring to the boil, then reduce the heat and simmer for 5–10 minutes, until reduced and very thick. Add the cherries and simmer for 5 minutes. Leave to cool a little.

**2** Thinly slice the tea buns and put a layer in the tin. Spoon half the cherry mixture roughly over them, firmly press another layer of tea bun on top, then the remaining cherries. Top with a final layer of tea bun slices, packing them firmly and closely together.

**3** Whisk together the eggs, sugar, milk, cream and vanilla and pour over the tea bun. Allow to stand for at least 5 minutes so the liquid is absorbed. Put the tin in a large baking dish. Pour water into the dish to come halfway up the sides of the tin. Bake for 1 hour 15 minutes, until a skewer

comes out clean when inserted into the centre. Cover with foil if browning too much. Cool completely in the tin. When cold, cut into squares and lift out with a spatula. Dust liberally with icing sugar to serve.

**Variation:** Try cinnamon or apple tea buns, Chelsea buns or even a large custard Danish pastry. They will slice easier if they are not completely fresh and have been refrigerated overnight.

*Add the cherries to the pan of juice and dissolved jam.*

*Spoon half the cherry mixture roughly over the sliced tea bun.*

*After pouring the cream mixture over the tea bun, leave it to be well absorbed.*

## REAL LEMON PIE

Preparation time: 25 minutes +
  overnight resting
Total cooking time: 50–55 minutes
Serves 8–10

1³/₄ **cups plain flour**
**pinch of salt**
**150 g chilled butter, cubed**
**2 tablespoons caster sugar**

*Lemon Filling*
**4 lemons**
**2 cups caster sugar**
**4 eggs**

**1 To make the Lemon Filling:**
Wash the lemons. Slice 2 unpeeled lemons very thinly (use a meat slicer if one is available); remove the seeds. Peel the remaining lemons and slice the flesh very thinly; remove the seeds and any white pith. Put the lemons in a bowl with the sugar and stir gently until all the slices are well coated. Cover and leave overnight.
**2** Preheat the oven to 180°C. Combine the flour and salt in a bowl. Rub in the butter until crumbly and stir in the sugar. Gradually add 1–2 tablespoons water, mixing with a knife. Press the dough together, divide in half and roll each portion into a 25 cm circle.

Lightly grease a 23 cm pie dish and line with a circle of pastry. Leave the other pastry circle flat; cover and chill.
**3** Beat the eggs and add to the lemon slices, mixing gently but thoroughly. Spoon into the pastry shell and cover with the pastry circle, crimping the edges to seal. Decorate the top with pastry scraps, brush with milk and then bake for 50–55 minutes, or until golden brown.

### COOK'S FILE

**Note:** Thick-skinned or tart lemons are ideal for this. If using ripe or thin-skinned lemons, you may need to reduce the sugar by ¹/₃ cup.

*Peel and remove the pith from two of the lemons and slice the flesh very thinly.*

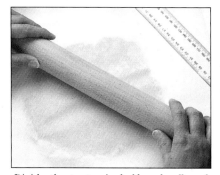

*Divide the pastry in half and roll each portion into a 25 cm circle.*

*Use a ladle to spoon the lemon filling into the pastry shell.*

## GRAPES WITH RED WINE ESPRESSO SAUCE AND SHORTBREADS

Preparation time: 25 minutes
Total cooking time: 25 minutes
Serves 4

1/4 cup brewed
     espresso coffee
1/2 cup good red wine
zest of 1 orange
4 cinnamon sticks
1 1/2 tablespoons honey
60 g butter
2 cups mixed grapes

*Shortbreads*
1 cup plain flour
1 cup rice flour
100 g chilled butter, chopped
2 tablespoons icing sugar
1 teaspoon grated orange rind
1 tablespoon orange juice

**1** Combine the coffee, wine, orange zest, cinnamon, honey and butter in a large frying pan. Simmer for about 10 minutes or until slightly thickened.
**2** Add the grapes and simmer for a further 3 minutes. Serve warm with Shortbreads and ice cream, cream or mascarpone cheese.
**3 To make Shortbreads:** Preheat the oven to 180°C. Put the flours, butter, icing sugar and rind in a food processor and process until fine and crumbly. Add the orange juice and 2–3 tablespoons of cold water and process until the mixture just comes together. Turn out onto a lightly floured surface, knead gently until smooth and then roll out. Cut out shapes with a biscuit cutter and bake on a greased oven tray for 15 minutes, or until pale golden. Cool slightly and dust with extra icing sugar if you like.

### COOK'S FILE

**Note:** Seedless grapes are obviously best for this recipe, if possible.

*Add the grapes to the coffee syrup and sauté for another 3 minutes.*

*Process the flour, butter, icing sugar and orange rind until crumbly.*

*Use a biscuit cutter to make Shortbreads in any shape.*

## CAPPUCCINO MOUSSE

Preparation time: 1 hour + chilling
Total cooking time: 5 minutes
Serves 6

250 g white chocolate
    melts, melted
125 g unsalted butter, melted
2 eggs, lightly beaten
3 teaspoons gelatine
300 ml thickened cream
3 teaspoons instant
    coffee powder
ground nutmeg, for
    decoration

**1** Mix together the chocolate, butter and eggs in a bowl and stir until smooth. Sprinkle the gelatine over 2 tablespoons water in a small bowl and stand this in a pan of simmering water, stirring until the gelatine has dissolved. Leave to cool slightly, before stirring into the chocolate mixture. Mix well and then cover and refrigerate for 30 minutes, or until just starting to set.
**2** Beat the cream into stiff peaks and gently fold into the mousse. Spoon about a third of the mousse into a separate bowl and set aside. Mix the coffee powder with 3 teaspoons hot water and fold into the remaining mousse.

**3** Spoon the coffee mousse evenly into 6 small glasses or dessert dishes and smooth the surface. Spoon or pipe the white mousse over the top and then sprinkle with nutmeg, cover and refrigerate for several hours or preferably overnight before serving.

### COOK'S FILE

**Note:** If white chocolate melts are not available, you can always use a slab of white chocolate, cut into chunks and melted, instead.
**Hint:** If at any stage the butter, chocolate, egg and gelatine mixture curdles, whisk in a little cream until it becomes smooth again.

*Sprinkle the gelatine over two tablespoons of water in a small bowl.*

*Add the cooled gelatine to the white chocolate mixture.*

*Mix the coffee with hot water and fold gently into the mousse.*

## CHERRY FRITTER MOUNTAIN

Preparation time: 45 minutes
Total cooking time: 30 minutes
Serves 4–6

1 cup plain flour
pinch salt
1/4 cup caster sugar
40 g butter, melted
3 egg whites

400 g fresh cherries, pitted
oil for deep frying
icing sugar, to dust

**1** Put the sifted flour, salt and sugar in a bowl, make a well in the centre and add the butter and 2/3 cup warm water. Gradually whisk together until smooth—if you can't get rid of the lumps you can strain the batter through a sieve. Cover and leave to stand for 30 minutes.
**2** Beat the egg whites until firm

peaks form, then fold into the batter.
**3** Dip the cherries in the batter with a spoon and deep-fry, a few at a time, draining on paper towels. Pile up into a mountain and serve warm, dusted with icing sugar.

### COOK'S FILE

**Note:** If fresh cherries are unavailable use canned pitted black cherries instead. Drain them well on paper towels and then coat them with cornflour before dipping in the batter.

*Gradually whisk the warm water and melted butter into the flour mixture.*

*Gently fold the egg whites into the batter, trying not to lose the volume.*

*Deep fry a few cherries at a time and drain them on paper towels.*

*Cappuccino Mousse (top) and Cherry Fritter Mountain*

## SUMMER BERRY TRIFLE

Preparation time: 40 minutes + chilling
Cooking time: 10 minutes + infusing
Serves 6

85 g packet raspberry jelly
1 sponge cake, cut into 2 layers
1/3 cup raspberry jam
1/3–1/2 cup sherry or orange juice
250 g raspberries
250 g blackberries or
   strawberries
250 g blueberries

*Custard Cream*
1 1/4 cups milk
1 vanilla bean
3 egg yolks
1/4 cup caster sugar
1 tablespoon custard powder
300 ml cream, lightly whipped

**1** Make the jelly, pour into a tin and chill until set. Chop roughly. Spread half the sponge with jam, sandwich together and cut into small cubes. Put in a bowl, sprinkle with sherry or orange juice and set aside.

**2 To make Custard Cream:** Heat the milk and vanilla bean in a pan until just starting to bubble. Remove from the heat, scrape the seeds from the bean, put seeds and bean back into the milk and leave to infuse for 20 minutes. Strain through muslin to remove the bean. Whisk together the egg yolks and sugar until thick and pale. Beat in the custard powder until smooth and whisk in the warm milk. Return to medium low heat and whisk until thickened and smooth. Cook for a further minute then cover and cool. Fold in the cream.

**3** Pour a little Custard Cream into the base of a 1.5 litre glass serving bowl and layer with cake, mixed berries and jelly. Repeat the layers. Put a thick layer of Custard Cream on top and chill for 2 hours or overnight. Top with swirls of extra whipped cream.

**COOK'S FILE**

**Note:** Vanilla beans are available from speciality food stores, or use 1 teaspoon vanilla essence instead.
• Frozen berries can be used instead, if fresh are not available.

*Layer the sponge with jam, cut into small cubes and put in a bowl.*

*Beat the custard powder into the egg yolk and sugar mixture.*

*Build up the layers of cake, berries and then jelly.*

## BANANA PUDDING WITH BUTTERSCOTCH SAUCE

Preparation time: 30 minutes
Total cooking time: 1 hour 40 minutes
Serves 6–8

150 g butter
3/4 cup soft brown sugar
1 1/2 cups self-raising flour
1/2 cup plain flour
1/2 teaspoon bicarbonate of soda
1/2 teaspoon ground nutmeg
1 teaspoon vanilla essence
2 eggs, lightly beaten
3/4 cup buttermilk
2 small ripe bananas, mashed

*Butterscotch Sauce*
120 g butter
1/2 cup soft brown sugar
1 cup condensed milk
1 1/3 cups cream

**1** Grease an 8-cup pudding basin and line the base with non-stick baking paper. Grease a sheet of foil, cover with a sheet of non-stick baking paper and make a pleat along the centre.
**2** Stir the butter and sugar over low heat until dissolved. Sift the combined flours, soda and nutmeg into a bowl and make a well in the centre. Add the butter mixture, vanilla, egg and buttermilk. Stir with a wooden spoon until smooth. Stir in the banana.

Spoon into the basin, cover with the paper and foil, paper side down, and secure with string. (If you have a lidded steamer, lay non-stick baking paper over the basin and secure the lid with clips.) Put the basin on a saucer in a large pan and add boiling water to come two-thirds of the way up the basin. Cover with a tight-fitting lid. Boil for 1 1/2 hours, until a skewer comes out clean. Do not boil dry. Leave for 5 minutes then turn out.
**3 To make the Sauce:** Stir the butter, sugar, condensed milk and cream over low heat until the sugar has dissolved. Bring to the boil, reduce the heat and simmer for 3–5 minutes. Serve hot over the pudding.

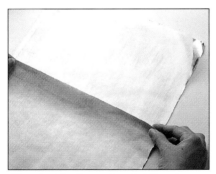

*The pleat in the centre of foil and paper allows it to expand during cooking.*

*Add the butter mixture, vanilla essence, eggs and buttermilk to the flour mixture.*

*Put the butter, sugar, condensed milk and cream in a pan and stir over low heat.*

# ORANGE PRALINE TORTE WITH MARSALA SAUCE

Preparation time: about 1 hour
Total cooking time: 1 hour 10 minutes
Serves 6

125 g unsalted butter
1/2 cup caster sugar
1 teaspoon grated orange rind
2 eggs
60 g white chocolate, melted and cooled
1/2 cup freshly squeezed orange juice
1 1/3 cups self-raising flour
2 tablespoons Marsala
300 ml thickened cream

*Orange Custard*
1/4 cup custard powder
1/4 cup caster sugar
1 cup milk
1 cup orange juice

*Praline*
1 cup pecans or almonds, toasted
1 cup caster sugar

*Marsala Cream Sauce*
1 1/2 cups thickened cream
1/3 cup Marsala
2 teaspoons honey
3 teaspoons cornflour

**1** Preheat the oven to 180°C. Grease and line the base of a deep, 20 cm round tin. Cream together the butter, sugar and rind until light and fluffy. Add the eggs one at a time, beating well each time; beat in the chocolate.
**2** Mix the orange juice with 2 tablespoons water; use a metal spoon to fold in spoonfuls of flour alternately with spoonfuls of juice. Spoon into the tin, smooth the surface and bake for 35–40 minutes, or until a skewer comes out clean when inserted into the centre. Cool on a wire rack.
**3** To make the Orange Custard: Combine the custard powder and sugar in a pan; gradually add the milk, stirring until smooth. Add the juice and stir until the mixture boils and thickens. Cover the surface with plastic wrap to prevent a skin forming and leave to cool to room temperature.
**4** Cut the cake into four layers. Brush one layer with a little Marsala, spread with a third of the orange custard, top with another cake layer and continue brushing with Marsala and spreading with custard until complete. Beat the cream into firm peaks and then spread over the cake. Chill until needed.
**5** To make Praline: Line a baking tray with non-stick baking paper and scatter with a single layer of pecans or almonds. Put the sugar in a small pan with 1/4 cup water. Stir over low heat until the sugar has dissolved. Bring to the boil, reduce the heat and simmer uncovered, without stirring, for about 8 minutes, or until a rich caramel colour. Pour immediately over the nuts on the tray and leave to cool. Break into pieces, process or crush and then arrange over the cake.
**6** To make the Marsala Cream Sauce: Put the cream and Marsala in a small pan and simmer, uncovered, for 5 minutes. Remove from the heat and add the honey. Mix the cornflour with 1 tablespoon water, add and stir over the heat until the sauce boils and thickens. Cool slightly and serve warm or chilled with sliced torte.

### COOK'S FILE

**Hint:** Torte best made a day in advance and decorated just before serving.

*Add the eggs one at a time, beating well after each addition.*

*Fold in spoonfuls of flour alternately with spoonfuls of orange juice.*

*Stir the orange custard continuously until it boils and thickens.*

Brush one layer of the cake with Marsala before spreading with orange custard.

Once the praline has cooled, break it into pieces or chop in a food processor.

Mix the cornflour with a little water and add to the sauce.

107

## VANILLA BAVAROIS

Preparation time: 40 minutes +
  overnight chilling
Total cooking time: 10–15 minutes
Serves 4

2³/4 cups milk
1 vanilla bean
1 cinnamon stick
6 egg yolks
²/3 cup caster sugar
3 teaspoons cornflour
3 teaspoons gelatine
³/4 cup cream
1 teaspoon vanilla essence

**1** Put the milk, vanilla bean and cinnamon in a pan and heat gently until almost boiling. Remove from the heat. Leave for 5 minutes to infuse. Remove the cinnamon stick and vanilla bean.

**2** Whisk together the egg yolks, sugar and cornflour until thick and pale. Gradually whisk in the milk. Pour into a large pan and stir continuously over low heat until the mixture just boils and thickens. Remove from the heat and cover the surface with plastic wrap to prevent a skin forming. Leave to cool a little.

**3** Dissolve the gelatine in 2 tablespoons of hot water and whisk into the custard. Beat the cream until soft peaks form and fold in with vanilla essence. Spoon into four 1-cup moulds. Tap the bases gently on a worktop to remove air bubbles. Chill overnight. To unmould, leave out of the fridge for 5 minutes then tilt the mould slightly on its side. Use your finger to gently pull the custard away from the edge, allowing air to enter and break the suction. A warm cloth wiped over the mould is often helpful too.

*Whisk the yolks, sugar and cornflour until thick and pale.*

*Gently tap the base of the mould on the bench to remove any air bubbles.*

*Use your finger to gently pull the set custard away from the edge of the mould.*

## MARINATED FIGS WITH RASPBERRY SAUCE

Preparation time: 20 minutes + 2 hours
Total cooking time: 10 minutes
Serves 4

1¼ cups dessert wine
1 cinnamon stick
1 tablespoon soft brown sugar
6 fresh figs, halved

300 g fresh raspberries
¼ cup caster sugar
1 teaspoon lemon juice
caster or soft brown sugar

**1** Warm together the wine, cinnamon and brown sugar. When the sugar has dissolved completely, remove from the heat and add the figs. Cover and leave to stand for 2 hours.

**2** Blend the raspberries in a food processor with the caster sugar. Press through a sieve to discard the seeds and then stir in the lemon juice.

**3** Lift out the figs with a slotted spoon and then strain and reserve the marinade. Put the figs on a foil-lined tray, sprinkle with a little caster or soft brown sugar and grill until just browned. Pour a little Sauce over the base of each plate then top with three fig halves. Brush with a little of the reserved marinade. Wonderful served with a dollop of mascarpone cheese.

*When the sugar has dissolved completely add the figs to the syrup.*

*Press the processed raspberries through a sieve to discard the seeds.*

*Remove the figs with a slotted spoon and place on a foil-lined tray.*

109

## CARAMEL RHUBARB CAKE

Preparation time: 40 minutes
Total cooking time: 55 minutes
Serves 6

1 cup sugar
250 g rhubarb, chopped
1 small Granny Smith apple,
    peeled, cored and sliced
2 eggs
1/3 cup icing sugar
1/2 teaspoon vanilla essence

100 g butter, melted and cooled
1 cup self-raising flour

**1** Preheat the oven to 180°C. Grease the base and side of a deep, 20 cm round cake tin and line the base with non-stick baking paper. Put the sugar in a pan with 1/3 cup water and heat gently, shaking occasionally, until dissolved. Increase the heat and cook until a pale caramel colour—it will turn a deeper colour in the oven. Pour into the tin and then press the rhubarb and apple into the caramel.

**2** Beat the eggs, sugar and vanilla essence until frothy. Fold in the melted butter. Sift the flour over the top and stir (the mixture will be soft). Spoon gently over the fruit, being careful not to dislodge it.

**3** Bake for about 45 minutes, or until set on top. Run a knife around the side of the cake and turn out very carefully onto a rack or plate. Best served warm with clotted cream.

### COOK'S FILE

**Hint:** If you don't turn the cake out straightaway the caramel will cool and make it stick to the tin.

*Press the pieces of apple and rhubarb into the caramel.*

*Beat the eggs, sugar and vanilla essence until they are frothy.*

*Run a knife around the outside of the cake to loosen it from the tin.*

# INDEX

# USEFUL INFORMATION

All our recipes are tested in the Australian Family Circle® Test Kitchen. Standard metric measuring cups and spoons approved by Standards Australia are used in the development of our recipes. All cup and spoon measurements are level. We have used 60 g (Grade 3) eggs in all recipes. Sizes of cans vary from manufacturer to manufacturer and between countries—use the can size closest to the one suggested in the recipe.

## Conversion Guide

| | |
|---|---|
| 1 cup | = 250 ml (8 fl oz) |
| 1 teaspoon | = 5 ml |
| 1 Australian tablespoon | = 20 ml (4 teaspoons) |
| 1 UK/US tablespoon | = 15 ml (3 teaspoons) |

NOTE: We have used 20 ml tablespoon measures. If you are using a 15 ml tablespoon, for most recipes the difference will not be noticeable. However, for recipes using baking powder, gelatine, bicarbonate of soda, small amounts of flour and cornflour, add an extra teaspoon for each tablespoon specified.

### Dry Measures
| | |
|---|---|
| 30 g | = 1 oz |
| 250 g | = 8 oz |
| 500 g | = 1 lb |

### Liquid Measures
| | |
|---|---|
| 30 ml | = 1 fl oz |
| 125 ml | = 4 fl oz |
| 250 ml | = 8 fl oz |

### Linear Measures
| | |
|---|---|
| 6 mm | = ¼ inch |
| 1 cm | = ½ inch |
| 2.5 cm | = 1 inch |

## Cup Conversions

| | |
|---|---|
| 1 cup biscuit crumbs | = 125 g (4 oz) |
| 1 cup plain flour | = 125 g (4 oz) |
| 1 cup self-raising flour | = 125 g (4 oz) |
| 1 cup caster sugar | = 250 g (8 oz) |
| 1 cup icing sugar | = 125 g (4 oz) |
| 1 cup jam | = 315 g (10 oz) |
| 1 cup honey | = 350 g (11 oz) |
| 1 cup sour cream | = 250 g (8 oz) |
| 1 cup sultanas | = 125 g (4 oz) |

## Oven Temperatures

Cooking times may vary slightly depending on the type of oven you are using. Before you preheat the oven, we suggest that you refer to the manufacturer's instructions to ensure proper temperature control.

| | °C | °F | Gas Mark |
|---|---|---|---|
| Very slow | 120 | 250 | ½ |
| Slow | 150 | 300 | 2 |
| Warm | 170 | 325 | 3 |
| Moderate | 180 | 350 | 4 |
| Mod. hot | 190 | 375 | 5 |
| Mod. hot | 200 | 400 | 6 |
| Hot | 220 | 425 | 7 |
| Very hot | 230 | 450 | 8 |

NOTE: For fan-forced ovens check your appliance manual, but as a general rule, set oven temperature to 20°C lower than the temperature indicated in the recipe.

## International Glossary

| | |
|---|---|
| almond meal | ground almons |
| buttercake mix | use sponge cake mix |
| choc bits | chocolate chips |
| compound chocolate | use cooking chocolate |
| raw sugar | demerara sugar |
| mango pulp | use mango purée |
| plain flour | all-purpose flour |

Published by Murdoch Books®, a division of Murdoch Magazines Pty Limited, 45 Jones Street, Ultimo NSW 2007.

**Managing Editor:** Jane Price. **Food Editors:** Kerrie Ray, Tracy Rutherford. **Editor:** Jane Price. **Designer:** Jackie Richards. **Recipe Development:** Amanda Cooper, Michelle Earl, Jennene Plummer, Kerrie Ray, Stephanie Souvilis, Dimitra Stais. **Home Economists:** Kerrie Mullins, Michelle Lawton, Michelle Earl, Wendy Goggin. **Photographers:** Chris Jones, Reg Morrison (Steps). **Food Stylist:** Mary Harris. **Food Preparation:** Kerrie Ray.

**CEO & Publisher:** Anne Wilson. **International Sales Director:** Mark Newman.

National Library of Australia Cataloguing-in-Publication Data. Cheesecakes, pavlovas and luscious desserts. Includes index. ISBN 0 86411 495 8. 1. Cheesecake (Cookery). 2. Desserts. 641.86. First printed 1996. Reprinted 1996, 1997, 1998 (twice). Printed by Prestige Litho, Queensland. PRINTED IN AUSTRALIA.

Australian distribution to supermarkets and newsagents by Gordon & Gotch Ltd, 68 Kingsgrove Road, Belmore, NSW 2192. Distributed in NZ by Golden Press, a division of HarperCollins Publishers, 31 View Road, Glenfield, PO Box 1, Auckland 1.

1 cm 2 cm 3 cm 4 cm 5 cm 6 cm 7 cm 8 cm 9 cm 10 cm 11 cm 12 cm 13 cm 14 cm 15 cm 16 cm 17 cm 18 cm 19 cm 20 cm 21 cm 22 cm 23 cm 24 cm 25 cm